REVELATION REVISITED

DR. NANCY HULSHULT

Revelation Revisited

ISBN: 979-8-9856988-8-6

Published by:
Narratus Creative | Narratus Press
P.O. Box 1413
Hamilton, OH 45012

Layout/Design: Narratus Creative | narratuscreative.com
Cover Photo Credits: Greg Schanding

Produced in the United States of America

Dedication & Appreciation

Thanks to Darrell Hulshult, for living by Philippians 4:8 as husband, father, grandfather, friend, and servant leader. *Finally, brothers and sisters, whatever is true, whatever is noble, whatever is right, whatever is pure, whatever is lovely, whatever is admirable—if anything is excellent or praiseworthy—think about such things.* —Philippians 4:8

Thanks to our sons, our daughters-in-love, and our grandchildren, who fuel our lives with love, laughter, tears, purpose, and hope for our next generations.

Thanks to Sheryl Burk, friend, editor, and literary consultant.

Thanks to contributing authors and friends for your testimonies, and to friends Pastor Rhonda Wirtley and Rev. Amy L. Arnold for your bookends of wisdom.

Thanks to Denise Chaney, publisher, NarratusCreative, friend, and author, *Unlikely Grace: This Is My Story, This Is My Song: Reflections, Revelations & Honest Questions for the Church I Love*.

Thanks to Debbie Day, friend and editor.

Thanks to Mary Lou Hudek, friend, editor, and member of **The Ukeladies**.

Thanks to Greg Schanding, friend and photographer for front and back covers.

Other Books by Nancy Hulshult

- I'm Still Here: From Cold War to COVID, Stories of My Spiritual Journey (2020)
    - Aún Sigo Aquí (Spanish Edition) (2021)
- Imagine You! 40 Days of Devotions: Finding Your Identity in God's Image (2021), co-author with Francesca King
    - ¡Imagínate A Ti!: 40 Días de Devociones: Encontrar Tu Identidad a Imagen de Dios (Spanish Edition) (2021)
- God's Restorative Nature (2022), co-author with Chad P. Shepherd
- The Manna God: 40 Days in Exodus (2023)
- Javelin Over Jericho: 24 Principles of Leadership from Joshua (2023)
- Bitter To Better: Do You Want To Be Made Well? (2024)
- Revelation Revisited (2024)

Foreword

by Rhonda Wirtley

Revelation?! The scariest, hardest to understand book in the Bible, right?! "I can't understand it, so I just don't read it" is a comment I've heard repeated over and over. I'll be honest, I've felt the same way! I've read it. I've read books about it, heard sermons, attended teaching conferences and yet, still struggled. But God wants us to read it! It's no less important than every other book of the Bible. God's Word is inspired, purposeful, and ALL of it is necessary and important.

Revelation 1:3 says, "Blessed is the one who reads aloud the words of this prophecy, and blessed are those who hear it and take to heart what is written in it……" I want God's blessings, and I know you do, too!

Enter "Revelation Revisited"! Revelation is the grand finish, the bookend to Genesis, and Nancy helps demystify it and makes it more comprehendible. She shines light into the dark places that are sometimes associated with Revelation. She walks with us through the hard to understand and challenges us to dig deeper. She replaces the scary with hope! To quote her, "Over and over in the history of his people, God has waited for repentance, has given second and third chances, and has spoken his intentions clearly to us all. He wants that none should perish, and he has been willing to wait for us to use our free will to believe in his Son, Jesus." That sums up a big part of Nancy's character. She wants to bring Jesus to the world and the world to Jesus!

The following are just some of the ways this study will help you understand Revelation better:

- The "Soul Survey" will help you look inward and recognize what your spiritual condition is.
- You'll have a better understanding about what was going on in the churches and what needed to change to help them (and us) live in closer relationship with God.

- You will have a clearer understanding of symbolism and numbers.
- Ties between scripture in the Old and New Testament with John's Revelation enlighten and explain.
- How'd I do? referenced scripture ties in with Revelation scripture to help give context.
- Honesty and integrity - Phrases like "presumably", "could represent" and "most likely" show Nancy's humbleness in presenting Revelation. She goes thoroughly through the scripture unraveling the truth.
- Application - This is how we truly learn, relating it to our lives.
- The extras - The way God/Jesus are interwoven through all of Revelation. The themes that break it down, give more intent, understanding.

Revelation can seem intimidating if you haven't read the rest of the Bible, especially if you don't have the Holy Spirit's guidance while reading it. Through this study, Nancy encourages us in ways that make it relevant and easier to learn. She asks thought provoking questions that inspire deep conversation for better understanding and challenges you to true introspection.

I know all of this to be true because I got to experience a Ladies' Retreat with Nancy teaching, sharing on this very subject. The Holy Spirit's anointing was obvious as she led us over the course of the retreat. Lives were changed! God showed up in a very palpable way! We laughed, we cried, we were happy, we were broken, and hope was restored, all because Nancy chose to bring Revelation to the forefront. She wasn't scared or intimidated, and she presented it in a way that stopped us from feeling that way, too. You see, God doesn't do anything halfway and neither has Nancy! She presents His Word in a way that reaches the lost, the newest believers, and challenges the seasoned believer.

My final words are going to be Nancy's, once again, because I believe if you see her heart, you will understand why she wrote this book and why it is important to read: "Make haste to repent. Make haste to share the Word of God with others. Make haste to follow all of God's instructions. Make haste in preparing for our last days, either our individual last days on earth or everyone's last days on earth with his second coming."

And this one sums Revelation up so well and the encouragement we can get by reading it: "The book of Revelation is a prophecy of hope, of promise, of the ongoing covenant between God and his people. It is a prophetic word of victory over sin, death, satan, the beast, and false prophets. Revelation is a reminder to live righteously and to refrain from idolatry, immorality, lies, and all sin. It is also a panoramic view of the magnitude of praise to God around this heavenly throne by the angels, saints, prophets, elders, and all living beings."

So, as you enter into the pages of "Revelation Revisited", enjoy journeying with Nancy on this God-ordained adventure!

Pastor Rhonda Wirtley
Executive Pastor
Trenton GracePointe Nazarene

TABLE OF CONTENTS

INTRODUCTION

I have read the Bible from cover to cover many times, and the last book has always been the most confusing, most fear-inducing book of them all. I scurried through the pages, looked up some commentaries, and ended up feeling lost in all the metaphors, prophetic figures, the world of spiritual warfare, and the controversial interpretations of Revelation. The first lesson I learned was that the title is "Revelation" rather than "Revelations." This book is one huge prophecy delivered to the apostle John on the island of Patmos, where he was in exile. The second lesson I learned was that the end of the story, the end of the Bible, ensured me that Jesus and his followers have the victory over sin, death, evil, Satan, the AntiChrist, and false prophets. Jesus has authority over all, and we will go with him when he returns for us in the final days of this earth. Knowing that Jesus defeats all wrongdoing gave me comfort and a new determination to live a righteous life, especially given all the "tribulations" that will come before the final victory.

I had an unhealthy fear of dying when I was younger. I don't know the cause or circumstances, but I always worried about my parents dying. Even when I went to college in upstate, Ohio, I thought that every phone call from home would be a call that one of my parents had passed. That never happened. Both of my parents lived well into their 90's, so a lifetime of worry was wasted on something that never happened. My fear of death may be part of the reason that I shied away from delving too deeply into end times, stories of Armageddon, and the book of Revelation. The end was near, and I didn't want to think about it.

As I grew older, I came to realize that my life was going to end one of two ways: (1) I would die and meet Jesus face to face on that day; or (2) Jesus would return and he would meet me and the rest of us all face to face. Either way, with the help of the Holy Spirit, I want to live a righteous life to be prepared for the second coming, my physical death (after having died to sin spiritually), and I want to take part in growing the number of believers in Jesus Christ.

Not until January 2024 did I receive a push from the Holy Spirit to revisit Revelation with a renewed mind and an open heart. I was surprised, because I had written three devotional books on Genesis, Exodus, and Joshua. I did not expect to jump to the end of the Bible for the next devotional, but the Holy Spirit showed me that Revelation is the bookend to Genesis. What God created from the beginning in its purest form he will restore in the end, purifying the earth, calling his people to a new heaven and earth, and purging the old earth of sin. After centuries of offering every people, nation, and language a chance to repent and to follow him, God finally closes the book on those who refuse to love him. He has sent and will send plagues and disastrous, miraculous world events that impact people directly. However, people continue to mock God in sinful, immoral, blasphemous ways.

It is strange to think of God finally losing hope in the lost, but after reading the Bible cover to cover, I am surprised that he didn't give up on humanity sooner. Over and over, God has forgiven, restored, and reset his people. He has reached out to all people, nations, and languages with the Word of Truth and the Testimony of his son, Jesus Christ. Finally, God will stop all creation and re-creation to establish his new heaven and earth. Revelation is an amazing testament to the patience and love of God for his people. In the very last chapters of Revelation, his covenant words are repeated. "I will be their God, and they will be my people," the same covenant he had established in Genesis and every book thereafter. It is the "happily ever after" ending to a love story begun and continued for eternity for his people.

> *1 Then I saw "a new heaven and a new earth," for the first heaven*
> *and the first earth had passed away, and there was no longer any sea.*
> *2 I saw the Holy City, the new Jerusalem, coming down out of heaven*
> *from God, prepared as a bride beautifully dressed for her husband.*
> *3 And I heard a loud voice from the throne saying, "Look! God's*
> *dwelling place is now among the people, and he will dwell with them.*
> *They will be his people, and God himself will be with them and be*
> *their God. 4 'He will wipe every tear from their eyes. There will be no*
> *more death' or mourning or crying or pain, for the old order of things*
> *has passed away."*

5 He who was seated on the throne said, "I am making everything new!" Then he said, "Write this down, for these words are trustworthy and true."

6 He said to me: "It is done. I am the Alpha and the Omega, the Beginning and the End. To the thirsty I will give water without cost from the spring of the water of life. 7 Those who are victorious will inherit all this, and I will be their God and they will be my children."
—Revelation 21:1-7

I realize that I need to give as much attention to understanding the last book of the Bible as I have given to the first. As a reader, and as one of God's people, I want closure. What finally happened to Adam and Eve after they sinned and were kicked out of the Garden of Eden, out of Paradise? After reading about all the descendants of the first humans to know and walk with God, wouldn't I want to read the fantastic ending where Paradise is restored and God's covenant with his people will come to pass?

Readers don't close the Bible feeling defeated, lost, or wondering what happened to the main characters. We read the last words with victory, hope, and praise to God for keeping his promises, his covenant of love for us.

Let's start at the beginning of the last book of the Bible and personalize our reading to better understand the message of the prophecy given to John. That journey begins now.

Chapter One

Revelation 1:1-3

The revelation from Jesus Christ, which God gave him to show his servants what must soon take place. He made it known by sending his angel to his servant John, who testifies to everything he saw—that is, the word of God and the testimony of Jesus Christ. Blessed is the one who reads aloud the words of this prophecy, and blessed are those who hear it and take to heart what is written in it, because ***the time is near.***

The prologue to John's book of Revelation declares in its first verse that "this is a revelation from Jesus Christ, which God gave him to show his servants the events that must soon take place."

The word "soon" is a relative concept, especially for God who always was, is, and will always be. When John tells the reader that "the time is near", surely his concept is different from God's concept of time, as well as our modern concept of time.

Raise your hand if you are guilty of becoming disgruntled when your fast food isn't in your hands and ready to be consumed soon enough. When you are asked to pull forward to wait for your order that will be ready soon, your aggravation increases just a bit more because you couldn't ask for, pay for, and receive your cooked food within minutes.

Perhaps you have heard stories passed down from your great grandparents about the harvest that would be ready "soon" after the planting season or when their homes would be heated shortly after they stoked the furnace with firewood.

Finally, tell any pregnant mother that it looks like her baby will be coming soon. More than not, she will answer, "Not soon enough!"

What is soon for one person or for God is different for another person. In the first book of the Bible, Genesis, when Joseph interpreted Pharaoh's dream about the seven years of great abundance in Egypt, followed by seven years of famine, Joseph declared that this prophecy would be fulfilled "soon". In this case, the abundance and the famine took place shortly after Joseph was promoted to "second in command" to Pharaoh to manage all the affairs of Egypt.

The reason the dream was given to Pharaoh in two forms is that the matter has been firmly decided by God, and God will do it soon.—Genesis 41:32

However, Jesus says, "I am coming soon" four times in Revelation, which was delivered centuries ago. In this prophecy, "soon" is the time frame of God delayed for when everyone has had the opportunity to become followers of Jesus Christ.

> *"I am coming soon. Hold on to what you have, so that no one will take your crown."*—Revelation 3:11
>
> *"Look, I am coming soon! Blessed is the one who keeps the words of the prophecy written in this scroll."*—Revelation 22:7
>
> *"Look, I am coming soon! My reward is with me, and I will give to each person according to what they have done."*—Revelation 22:12
>
> *He who testifies to these things says, "Yes, I am coming soon." Amen. Come, Lord Jesus.*—Revelation 22:20

Some Bible scholars have analyzed historical times to predict when Jesus will come again "soon".

In Mark 13, Jesus speaks prophetically about the destruction of the temple and signs of the end times. He predicts that there will be wars, nations against nations, earthquakes, famines, and persecutions. However, when his disciples ask him about the specific time, Jesus responds that even he does not know.

> *But about that day or hour no one knows, not even the angels in heaven, nor the Son, but only the Father. Be on guard! Be alert! You do not know when that time will come. It's like a man going away: He leaves his house and puts his servants in charge, each with their assigned task, and tells the one at the door to keep watch.*
>
> *Therefore keep watch because you do not know when the owner of the house will come back—whether in the evening, or at midnight, or when the rooster crows, or at dawn. If he comes suddenly, do not let him find you sleeping. What I say to you, I say to everyone: 'Watch!'"*—Mark 13:32-37

Also in Mark 13, Jesus uses the same language that he and his disciples had read in Isaiah 13 and Isaiah 34, as well as his language in his message to John in Revelation about the darkening of the sun, the sending of the angels, and the coming of the Son of Man.

> *If the Lord had not cut short those days, no one would survive. But for the sake of the elect, whom he has chosen, he has shortened them. At that time*

> *if anyone says to you, 'Look, here is the Messiah!' or, 'Look, there he is!' do not believe it. For false messiahs and false prophets will appear and perform signs and wonders to deceive, if possible, even the elect. So be on your guard; I have told you everything ahead of time.*
>
> *But in those days, following that distress,*
> *'the sun will be darkened,*
> *and the moon will not give its light;*
> *the stars will fall from the sky,*
> *and the heavenly bodies will be shaken.'*
>
> *At that time people will see the Son of Man coming in clouds with great power and glory. And he will send his angels and gather his elect from the four winds, from the ends of the earth to the ends of the heavens.*—Mark 13:20-26

Rather than focusing on how soon the prophecy is to be fulfilled, we should focus on God's reason for his delay: his elect, his chosen. Throughout the Bible, God has delayed judgment for the sake of saving his people. The accounts of Noah, Moses, Nineveh, and others show how much patience God exercises for the sake of his people repenting and turning back to him.

Considering that we will never know the exact time, that God is delaying his judgment for more people to follow him, and that Jesus has warned us to be on our guard, we should be mainly concerned about leading a righteous life following Jesus Christ and encourage others to do the same while there is still time.

With that in mind, we receive a blessing for sharing this prophecy and for listening to its message.

> *Blessed is the one who reads aloud the words of this prophecy, and blessed are those who hear it and take to heart what is written in it, because the time is near.*—Revelation 1:3

Revelation 1:4-8

In the opening verse of Revelation, the message is described as "a revelation". Then in verse 4, the message is described as a "letter from John to the seven churches in the province of Asia." John immediately attempted to deliver to the churches what was prophesied through him by greeting the seven churches in the province of Asia with the words of grace and peace. John wrote in the same salutary style as Paul began his letters to the Romans, Corinthians, Galatians, Ephesians, Philippians, Colossians, Thessalonians, Timothy, Titus, and Philemon, and as well as how Peter began his first and second letter.

Paul writes the exact greeting in Romans, Corinthians, Galatians, Ephesians, Philippians in this way: "Grace and peace to you from God our Father and from the Lord Jesus Christ." In the other letters, Paul's words are similar, other than adding "mercy" to the grace and peace in his letter to Timothy. Peter used grace and peace with a bit more flair:

> *Grace and peace be yours in abundance.*—1 Peter 1:2

> *Grace, mercy and peace from God the Father and from Jesus Christ, the Father's Son, will be with us in truth and love.*—2 Peter 1:2

John used similar wording when he wrote:

> *Grace, mercy and peace from God the Father and from Jesus Christ, the Father's Son, will be with us in truth and love.*—2 John 1:3

However, when John wrote Revelation, after hearing all the descriptors of God, he used the descriptors of God and Jesus as they were presented throughout the prophecy delivered to him:

> *Grace and peace to you from the one who is, who always was, and who is still to come; from the sevenfold Spirit before his throne; and from Jesus Christ. He is the faithful witness to these things, the first to rise from the dead, and the ruler of all the kings of the world.*—Revelation 1:4-5

John continues to praise and edify Jesus through the next three verses:

> *To him who loves us and has freed us from our sins by his blood, and has made us to be a kingdom and priests to serve his God and Father—to him be glory and power for ever and ever! Amen.*
> *"Look, he is coming with the clouds,"*
> *and "every eye will see him,*
> *even those who pierced him";*
> *and all peoples on earth "will mourn because of him."*
> *So shall it be! Amen.*

> *"I am the Alpha and the Omega," says the Lord God, "who is, and who was, and who is to come, the Almighty."*—Revelation 1:6-8

John had lived with Jesus, traveled with him, then was present at his crucifixion, resurrection, and ascension into heaven. Exiled because of his faith, John saw Jesus in yet another form in this revelation from heaven that was so clear, so precise, so amazing, that John was able to remember and write it all down. What an honor and a huge responsibility for one person to deliver this message to the seven churches and to the world! Jesus trusted John to be able to convey the Lord's messages of warnings, of affirmations, of victory, and of hope for those who would listen and continue to follow Jesus.

In verse 1 and 2, John described himself as being God's faithful servant:

> *The revelation from Jesus Christ, which God gave him to show his servants what must soon take place. He made it known by sending his angel to his servant John, who testifies to everything he saw—that is, the word of God and the testimony of Jesus Christ. Blessed is the one who reads aloud the words of this prophecy, and blessed are those who hear it and take to heart what is written in it, because the time is near.*—Revelation 1:1-3

The two components that demonstrate evidence of being a faithful servant of God: (1) the word of God, and (2) the testimony of Jesus Christ. Both the Word and the testimony of Jesus are to be read, spoken, heard, and taken to heart, that is, believed with our whole hearts.

In verse 6, John described Jesus' followers as "a Kingdom of priests for God the Father."

In verse 9, John describes himself as a brother and partner suffering and patiently enduring in God's kingdom as he was exiled for preaching and testifying about Jesus, that is, preaching the word of God and giving testimony about Jesus.

> *I, John, your brother and companion in the suffering and kingdom and patient endurance that are ours in Jesus, was on the island of Patmos because of the word of God and the testimony of Jesus.*—Revelation 1:9

Following his introductory greeting and statement of purpose and praise to the Lord, John described the setting for this vision of Jesus and this prophecy. He was worshiping in the Spirit when a loud voice suddenly blasted behind him.

> *On the Lord's Day I was in the Spirit, and I heard behind me a loud voice like a trumpet.*—Revelation 1:10

If you enjoy imagining John's experience, if you love to live vicariously through other people, then be prepared to cover your ears! The book of Revelation is LOUD: loud voices, loud trumpet blasts, loud praise, earthquakes and blasts of thunder. Except for 30 minutes of complete silence, there is no "still, small voice of God" like Elijah heard in 1 Kings 19 after an earthquake, a strong wind, and a fire (yes, "earth, wind, and fire"). In your imagination, turn on your decibel meter as you read the sheer volume that is described in Revelation.

No still, small voices for John in this visit from God! John would have no trouble hearing what he was commanded to write and to pass on to the world, because he was not to leave out a single word. In Revelation 22, God warned John (and all of us):

I warn everyone who hears the words of the prophecy of this scroll: If anyone adds anything to them, God will add to that person the plagues described in this scroll. And if anyone takes words away from this scroll of prophecy, God will take away from that person any share in the tree of life and in the Holy City, which are described in this scroll.—Revelation 22:18-19

As you read the following list of loud communications in Revelation, remember to turn an ear to the noise level, and live vicariously through John.

- *voice like the sound of rushing waters - 1:15*
- *loud voice proclaiming - 5:2*
- *voice like a trumpet - 4:1*
- *flashes of lightning, rumblings and peals of thunder - 4:5, 8:5, 11:19 (+hailstorm), 16:18 (+earthquake)*
- *loud voice of many angels, numbering thousands upon thousands, and ten thousand times ten thousand - 5:11-12*
- *every creature in heaven and on earth and under the earth and on the sea, and all that is in them, saying - 5:13*
- *loud voice of thunder - 6:1*
- *loud voice - 6:10, 7:2, 7:9, 8:13, 12:9, 14:7, 14:9, 14:15, 14:18, 16:1,*

16:17, 18:2, 19:17, 21:3

- *great earthquake - 6:12, 11:13*
- *trumpets sounding - 8:7, 8:8, 8:10, 8:12, 9:1, 9:13, 11:15*
- *voices of the seven thunders - 10:3*
- *war broke out - 12:7, 12:17*
- *roar of rushing waters and like a loud peal of thunder of harpists - 14:2, 19:6*
- *exclaim - 18:18*
- *roar of a great multitude in heaven shouting - 19:1*
- *shouted - 19:3*
- *cried out - 19:4*

The first words John heard were in the form of an order: to write in a book everything he saw and send it to the seven churches. Only when he turned to see the vision of Jesus as the Son of Man did he fall to his feet "as if I were dead" (verse 17), but Jesus laid his right hand on John and told him not to be afraid. Although Jesus had been glorified in heaven, John was able to feel Jesus' hand on him. Jesus identified himself and then proceeded with his initial instruction:

When I saw him, I fell at his feet as if I were dead. Then he placed his right hand on me and said: "Do not be afraid. I am the First and the Last. I am the Living One; I was dead, and now look, I am alive for ever and ever! And I hold the keys of death and Hades. "Write down what you have seen –both the things that are happening and the things that will happen."—Revelation 1:17-19

In Revelation 1:12-16, John paints a detailed picture of Jesus, the Son of Man, standing in the middle of seven golden lampstands. He is wearing a long robe, gold sash with seven stars in his right hand. His physical features are described as head and hair white as wool, eyes like flames of fire, feet like polished bronze refined in a furnace, a thundering voice, a face as brilliant as the sun, and a mouth with a sharp two-edged sword.

John would be one of three disciples most suited to receive this vision of Jesus glorified in brilliance within the heavenly realm. In the gospels of Matthew, Mark, and Luke, when Jesus was transfigured with Moses and Elijah, the disciples (Peter, James and John) had already seen Jesus' face as bright as the sun and his clothes whiter than white.

> *His face shone like the sun, and his clothes became as white as the light.* —Matthew 17:2

In Revelation 1:20, Jesus explains to John that the seven stars are the angels or the messengers of the seven churches, and the seven lampstands are the seven churches. The two-edged sword in Jesus' mouth signifies the Word of God that can cut quickly to the soul or the Word of God that can both bless and curse. Jesus' feet looking like polished bronze "refined in a furnace" could be an allusion to Daniel 3 when the person "like the son of man" walked in the fire with Shadrach, Mesach, and Abednego when they refused to bow down to anyone but God.

John's use of parallelism is remarkable. First, he repeats the opening line beginning with the words, "To the angel of the church..." Then he follows this parallel sentence with a different specific descriptor of Jesus that aligns with his warning or promise for each church. There is a range of good news for the victorious and not so good news for those who continue to miss the mark. John reinforces each message to the seven churches by the words he chooses to describe Jesus. John's parallel writing style shows the brilliance of his recall of the Revelation, his skillful authorship, and his ability to connect the qualities of Jesus to His message for each church.

Church in Ephesus - Parallel of Lampstands

> *"To the angel of the church in Ephesus write: These are the words of him who holds the seven stars in his right hand and walks among the seven golden lampstands."*—Revelation 2:1

The stars are his angels overseeing the churches, and the lampstands represent the churches. In Revelation 2:5, Jesus threatens to remove their lampstand if they don't repent. The purpose of a lampstand is to hold the light. In essence, If the church of Ephesus did not repent and shine the light of Jesus, then Jesus would remove the church. Not only was Jesus issuing a strong warning, he was also emphasizing the purpose of the church: to be the light of Jesus to the world. He walks among the lampstands and has authority over them.

CHURCH IN SMYRNA: PARALLEL OF DEATH AND LIFE

To the angel of the church in Smyrna write: These are the words of him who is the First and the Last, who died and came to life again.—Revelation 2:8

In Revelation 2:10-11, Jesus tells those who will suffer and die for their faith that they will not be harmed when he comes again to judge the world, the second death.

> *Do not be afraid of what you are about to suffer. I tell you, the devil will put some of you in prison to test you, and you will suffer persecution for ten days. Be faithful, even to the point of death, and I will give you life as your victor's crown. Whoever has ears, let them hear what the Spirit says to the churches. The one who is victorious will not be hurt at all by the final judgment of the second death.*—Revelation 2:10-11

Jesus, the one who died and came to life, promises that the victorious will not be harmed by the second death, also described in Revelation 21:8

> *But the cowardly, the unbelieving, the vile, the murderers, the sexually immoral, those who practice magic arts, the idolaters and all liars—they will be consigned to the fiery lake of burning sulfur. This is the second death.*
> —Revelation 21:8

CHURCH IN PERGAMUM: PARALLEL OF THE SWORD

"To the angel of the church in Pergamum write: These are the words of him who has the sharp, double-edged sword."—Revelation 2:12

Jesus says that they should repent or he will come to them suddenly and fight against them with the sword of his mouth.

CHURCH IN THYATIRA: PARALLEL OF METALS

"To the angel of the church in Thyatira write: These are the words of the Son of God, whose eyes are like blazing fire and whose feet are like burnished bronze.—Revelation 2:18

Jesus promises to give the victorious one the authority to rule the nations with an iron rod and smash them like clay pots (under their feet). He warns against tolerating Jezebel, a false prophet, who leads followers to practice sexual immorality and idol worship.

This image of Jesus' blazing eyes of fire and feet of burnished bronze fortifies his transfer of authority with iron to smash the clay pots of idols and idol worshippers. The action of "smashing" was used in Deuteronomy 7 when God's people were to enter the Promised Land and smash the altars and idols of the nations there. In 2 Chronicles 34:4, Josiah smashes false gods to pieces.

> *Under his direction the altars of the Baals were torn down; he cut to pieces the incense altars that were above them, and smashed the Asherah poles and the idols. These he broke to pieces and scattered over the graves of those who had sacrificed to them.*—2 Chronicles 34:4

Years ago I was ordained as a minister in the Church of God when I was the principal of a Christian school. When the school closed, I worked in public schools and asked God why I was not called to another Christian school or to a church for ministry. In my prayer time, the Lord told me that I had a new calling. I was to become a "Pastor of Broken Pieces," a name that described my new purpose for the next 25 years, particularly in alternative education. However, my own family has gone through times of "Broken Peaces." We waited and prayed for God to mend us, and we trusted him for the blessings through the brokenness. The Lord will break us if we won't bend our knees, but he will restore us if we do. The Word is clear in Revelation 2:8 but also in Isaiah 45:9 and Lamentations 4:2.

> *"Woe to those who quarrel with their Maker, those who are nothing but potsherds among the potsherds on the ground. Does the clay say to the potter, 'What are you making?' Does your work say, 'The potter has no hands'?*—Isaiah 45:9

> *How the precious children of Zion, once worth their weight in gold, are now considered as pots of clay, the work of a potter's hands!*—Lamentations 4:2

Church of Sardis - Parallel of Stars and Angels

> *"To the angel of the church in Sardis write: These are the words of him who holds the seven spirits of God and the <u>seven stars</u>.*—Revelation 3:1

Jesus warns them to wake up, that they are almost dead spiritually, or he will come as a thief. For the victorious, Jesus will never erase their names from the Book of Life and will announce before his Father and <u>his angels</u> that they are his. Remember that the seven stars are the angels.

CHURCH OF PHILADELPHIA - PARALLEL OF KEYS

> *To the angel of the church in Philadelphia write: These are the words of him who is holy and true, who holds the key of David. What he opens no one can shut, and what he shuts no one can open.* — Revelation 3:7

Jesus says that he has opened a door for them that no one can close. He promises to protect them from the great time of testing and that they will be citizens in the city of his God - the new Jerusalem. They are essentially given the keys to the city.

CHURCH OF LAODICEA - PARALLEL OF RULERS

> *"To the angel of the church in Laodicea write: These are the words of the Amen, the faithful and true witness, the ruler (source, beginning) of God's creation.* — Revelation 3:14

Jesus promises the victorious that they will sit with him on his throne, just as he was victorious and sat with his Father on his throne.

In the next chapters, we will look at each of the seven churches through our own lens to see what Jesus expects of all of us and what he will not tolerate from us.

To personalize the messages to the churches, here's a "soul poll" to check our own spiritual conditions at this moment.

Reflection

My Soul Survey from Revelation

Directions: read each statement and decide which ONE most accurately describes your current spiritual condition and check the box.

☐ **I am working hard, persevering, but I have lost the passion that I had for Jesus when I first decided to follow Him. (Ephesus)**

☐ **I am suffering afflictions, and I am depleted of resources. (Smyrna)**

☐ **I am a faithful follower of Jesus but have been living with one foot in Christianity and one foot in the worldly culture without a strict separation. (Pergamum)**

☐ **I am loving, faithful, serving and persevering, doing more even than I did when I first became a follower of Jesus, but I have tolerated false prophets, false teachers, or false teachings. (Thyatira)**

☐ **I have a reputation of being spiritually alive to others, but I am really spiritually dead inside. My deeds are unfinished in the sight of God, and I need a "reset" to strengthen what love and faith I do have. (Sardis)**

☐ **I am enduring patiently with little strength, but I have kept my faith and have not denied the name of Jesus. (Philadelphia)**

☐ **I am spiritually lukewarm and independent, telling people that I am rich or blessed and don't need a thing, but in God's eyes, I am really wretched, pitiful, poor, blind, and naked. I need to be refined in the fire of His Holy Spirit and to purify myself so that I can see clearly what I need to be for Jesus. (Laodicea)**

☐ **None of the above statements describe my spiritual condition, which is ____**

Thematically, the book of Revelation is a study of the character and identity of God, a study of the nature of God in the Trinity: God, the Father, Jesus, the Son, and the Holy Spirit. A recurring description of God is that he is eternal and exists with no beginning and no end. His authority is established as he declares that he is the Alpha and Omega, the first and the last. All of creation begins and ends with him,and all authority begins and ends with him. Because God has created all things and has authority over all things, God also has the right to pass judgment over all things. God can save, and God can destroy.

Within the identity of God is his Son, Jesus Christ, the Messiah. God sent his Son to save his creation from sin and death. By dying on the cross for our sin, Jesus assumed authority over death, rose from the grave, and ascended into heaven to regain his seat on the throne of heaven with and as God. He has made his people as priests in his kingdom to serve him.

Twice in Revelation 1:4-8, God is identified as the one who is, and who was, and who is to come. God is timeless; his existence has no beginning nor end; and he is ever-present with us. He was here before us; he is with us; and he will be with us forever. There is nothing that God doesn't know about us; there is nothing that God still needs to learn about us. We can be fully open to him because there is nothing that we could hide from him anyway. He was here at our birth; here with us now; and will be here with us when we transition from this earth to his new earth and heavenly home. Because God knows us so fully, we want to know him fully. Therefore, we seek to communicate with him, to study his Word of Truth, and to know more about his character and identity. Who is this eternal friend of ours, and why does he want a relationship with us?

In Revelation 1:5, Jesus is the Christ, the Messiah and Redeemer. In Greek, he is Cristos, "the anointed one". Jesus is the appointed, anointed Son of God.

Jesus is the faithful witness, the constant one who has the personal experience of being in heaven with God the Father. He is the one who gave first-hand testimony to the world of his love for us through his sacrifice on the cross. He is the one who taught us how to love, how to serve, and how to know God. He stayed true to his mission on earth from his humble birth to his glorious ascension into heaven. Jesus is THE witness who showed his disciples the way, the truth, and the life.

Jesus is the firstborn from the dead. He is the firstborn Son of God, the firstborn son of Mary, and the firstborn from the grave. He defeated death through his resurrection from the grave, as he foretold his disciples.

Jesus is the ruler of the kings of the earth. Jesus has full authority over any earthly authority. He had the authority on earth to forgive sins, to heal, to drive out evil spirits, and to transfer his authority to his disciples to do the same. Jesus will defeat any ruler who comes against him in the spiritual realm in heaven and on earth.

Jesus loves us. Jesus loves us for who we are, created by God and heirs with him to God's throne. Jesus values us and is in a loving relationship with us. Whether or not we receive his love is up to us. He still loves.

Jesus freed us from our sins by his blood. When a sacrifice was required to God as atonement for sin, animal sacrifices had been offered time and again as his people came before him in his temple. As the "once and for all" sacrifice, God offered his Son, Jesus, in atonement for sin for all people for all time. Jesus freed us to gain access to heaven, to the throne of God. By his stripes, we are healed.

Jesus made us a kingdom and priests to serve God his Father. Jesus elevated us to be a part of the community of believers in the kingdom of God with Jesus as our King and with us as priests to serve God, his Father. What a privilege to be raised to the status of priests! What an honor to be able to serve God, who does not need our service but who desires our servanthood! Jesus made that happen! Jesus served because he loved. We are to do the same. Jesus shed his blood to raise us to be royal blood in the kingdom with him. Who wouldn't want to be a part of this amazing move of God?

In Revelation 1:7, when Jesus comes with the clouds of heaven, everyone will see him, even those who pierced and crucified him! All nations will mourn for him. His identity and truth will be revealed to all, those who believe in Him and those who reject Him.

In Revelation 1:8, God is the Alpha and Omega, the first and the last. God is Lord, the Lord of all heavenly and earthly creation. God is Almighty, all powerful, able to do all things and to power over all things. God is, and was, and is to come.

In the description of the Alpha and Omega, there is a linear image of a first to last. In the description of "is, was, and is to come", there is a timeless image of eternity that stretches our human imaginations. God is a timeless being who transfers that opportunity to us to be with him for eternity. To be in an eternal relationship with God elevates us from our past sinful beings to an eternal state of "forgiven and free"!

> *Grace and peace to you from him* ***who is, and who was, and who is to come,*** *and from the seven spirits before his throne, and from Jesus Christ, who is the faithful witness, the firstborn from the dead, and the ruler of the kings of the earth.*
>
> *To him who loves us and has freed us from our sins by his blood, and has made us to be a kingdom and priests to serve his God and Father—to him be glory and power for ever and ever! Amen.*
>
> *"Look, he is coming with the clouds,"*
> *and "every eye will see him,*
> *even those who pierced him";*
> *and all peoples on earth "will mourn because of him."*
> *So shall it be! Amen.*
>
> *"I am the* ***Alpha and the Omega,"*** *says the* ***Lord God, "who is, and who was, and who is to come, the Almighty."***— Revelation 1:4-8

In Revelation 1:17-18, Jesus identifies himself as the First and the Last, just as God identifies as the First and the Last, the Alpha and the Omega.

Jesus declares that he is the Living One, once dead but now alive for eternity.

Jesus holds the keys of death and Hades. He conquered the grave himself, and he has the victory over Satan, the beast, and false prophets, who will be sent to Hades at the final judgment. (Hades was known as the Greek god of the dead.)

> *When I saw him, I fell at his feet as though dead. Then he placed his right hand on me and said: "Do not be afraid. I am the First and the Last. I am the Living One; I was dead, and now look, I am alive for ever and ever! And I hold the keys of death and Hades.* — Revelation 1:17-18

The book of Revelation speaks of God's word and the testimony of Jesus Christ. When Jesus' disciples professed the word of God and gave the testimony of Jesus Christ, they were repeating what they had been taught. They were fulfilling the great commission given to them by Jesus himself.

> *Therefore go and make disciples of all nations, baptizing them in the name of the Father and of the Son and of the Holy Spirit, 20 and teaching them to obey everything I have commanded you. And surely I am with you always, to the very end of the age."* — Matthew 28:19-20

The spoken word of God and the words of Jesus Christ are to be repeated by God's people and the disciples of Jesus. We are to know and speak the Word of God, and we are to speak the testimony of Jesus to all people. That is our purpose; that is our commission by Jesus before he ascended into heaven. Because of the Word and the Testimony, disciples of Jesus have been martyred for their faith. Not only were 11 of the 12 disciples killed for their testimonies, people in the modern world continued to be martyred for their faith.

The book of Revelation emphasizes the importance of maintaining our faith in the Word of God and the testimony of Jesus, even to the point of death, if necessary. However, all who remain faithful will be rewarded, as promised. Revelation, itself, is a testimony given to John by Jesus for the churches.

CHAPTER TWO

Revelation 2

The second chapter of Revelation covers the messages to four of the seven churches: Ephesus, Smyrna, Pergamum, and Thyatira.

REVELATION 2:2-7 MESSAGE TO THE CHURCH IN EPHESUS

Jesus says that he knows all the things they do and has seen their hard work and patient endurance. They have not tolerated evil people and have tested false prophets. However, Jesus' complaint towards the church is a warning.

> *Yet I hold this against you: You have forsaken the love you had at first. Consider how far you have fallen! Repent and do the things you did at first. If you do not repent, I will come to you and remove your lampstand from its place.*—Revelation 3:11

After the warning comes hope and reward for those who are victorious.

> *To the one who is victorious, I will give the right to eat from the tree of life, which is in the paradise of God.*—Revelation 2:7

REVELATION 2:2-7 MESSAGE TO THE CHURCH IN EPHESUS

Jesus says that he knows about their suffering and poverty, but he says that they are rich. He tells the people of the church in Smyrna not to be afraid of what they are about to suffer, that is, being thrown into prison to test them for ten days. If they remain faithful, even when facing death, Jesus will give them the crown of life. Whoever is victorious will not be harmed by the second death.

This is the first time in Revelation that Satan and the devil are mentioned. The terms Satan and the devil are used interchangeably, but this enemy has an identity as a former angel of heaven. He is not a red cartoon character with a pitchfork, horns, and a pointed tail, nor is he a movie protagonist or antagonist. He is not a figment of one's imagination nor just a metaphor for evil. He is a being, a power, a former angel of heaven rebelling against God in his presence on earth. He can gain control over people, who choose to follow him instead of God. To clarify his identity, let us jump ahead to Revelation 12 for the description of the origin of his presence on earth.

> *Then war broke out in heaven. Michael and his angels fought against the*

> *dragon, and the dragon and his angels fought back. But he was not strong enough, and they lost their place in heaven. The great dragon was hurled down—that ancient serpent called the devil, or Satan, who leads the whole world astray. He was hurled to the earth, and his angels with him.*
> —Revelation 12:7-9

To the church in Smyrna, Jesus shows us that Satan does have the power to test us, but we have the ultimate victory through Jesus if we remain faithful.

> *I know your afflictions and your poverty—yet you are rich! I know about the slander of those who say they are Jews and are not, but are a synagogue of Satan. Do not be afraid of what you are about to suffer. I tell you, the devil will put some of you in prison to test you, and you will suffer persecution for ten days. Be faithful, even to the point of death, and I will give you life as your victor's crown. Whoever has ears, let them hear what the Spirit says to the churches. The one who is victorious will not be hurt at all by the second death.*—Revelation 2:9-10

Revelation 2:12-17 Message to the Church in Pergamum

Jesus acknowledges that they live in the city where Satan has his throne, yet they have remained loyal to Jesus, even when Antipas was martyred there.

> *I know where you live—where* ***Satan*** *has his throne. Yet you remain true to my name. You did not renounce your faith in me, not even in the days of Antipas, my faithful witness, who was put to death in your city—where* ***Satan*** *lives.*—Revelation 2:13

Jesus deplores the tolerance of the sin of eating food offered to idols and of living in sexual sin. He calls for repentance or he will come suddenly and fight against the false prophets, the Nicolaitans, with the sword of his mouth. This sword could mean his judgment that comes from the truth of God's Word coming from the mouth of Jesus. To the victorious, Jesus promises the gift of some of the manna hidden away in heaven, as well as a white stone on which will be engraved a new name that no one understands, except the one who receives it.

> *Whoever has ears, let them hear what the Spirit says to the churches. To the one who is* ***victorious,*** *I will give some of the hidden manna. I will also give that person a white stone with a new name written on it, known only to the one who receives it.*—Revelation 2:17

The manna signifies the daily provision that God had given to the Israelites when they wandered the desert for 40 years. The gift from Jesus of a white stone with a new name signifies an intimate relationship between the Lord and the faithful, an understanding that only exists between Jesus and the one who receives the stone.

REVELATION 2:18-29 MESSAGE TO THE CHURCH IN THYATIRA

Jesus applauds their love, faith, service, patient endurance, and constant improvement in all these things. However, they are permitting the false prophet, Jezebel, to lead Jesus' servants astray. After giving her time to repent, Jesus sees that she does not want to repent, so he will throw her on a bed of suffering, along with those who commit adultery with her. Jesus will give the adulterers time to repent as well, but if not, then he will strike her children dead.

Jesus shows his capacity to forgive and to condemn. After this show of judgment upon Jezebel and her partners, Jesus declares his ability to see deeply into the hearts and minds of everyone in order to give each what is deserved.

> *Then all the churches will know that I am he who searches hearts and minds, and I will repay each of you according to your deeds.*—Revelation 2:23

Jesus admonishes his followers to hold on to the truth from him and not to learn the so-called deep secrets, or deeper truths, of Satan. Jesus promises the victorious the authority over all the nations, the same authority given to him by the Father.

> *Now I say to the rest of you in Thyatira, to you who do not hold to her teaching and have not learned* ***Satan's*** *so-called deep secrets, 'I will not impose any other burden on you, except to hold on to what you have until I come.' To the one who is* ***victorious*** *and does my will to the end, I will give authority over the nations— that one 'will rule them with an iron scepter and will dash them to pieces like pottery'—just as I have received authority from my Father.*—Revelation 2:24-26

Jesus also promises to give them the "morning star!" Being given the "morning star" could mean that the victorious would have the authority to crush the nations and Satan himself. The "morning star," noted in Isaiah 14:12, refers to the angel fallen from heaven. Jesus is referred to as the bright morning star in Revelation 22:16. In the context of the faithful receiving the authority to smash the nations like clay pots, Jesus, here, is likely referencing the authority the victorious will have over Isaiah's "morning star," Satan.

Thematically, regarding the nature and identity of God in the Trinity, the second chapter of Revelation focuses heavily on Jesus, the Son of God.

In Revelation 2:1, In the message to the church in Ephesus, Jesus holds the seven stars in the right hand, who are presumed to be the seven angels of the seven churches. Jesus walks among the seven golden lampstands that are presumably the seven churches. It is fitting that Jesus, as the light of the world, walks among lampstands, that is, the pillars or menorahs used to give light (Hebrew "to flame") to the priests who work in the Holy Place of the tabernacle. Churches are given the responsibility to shine the light of God to the world.

> *These are the words of him who holds the seven stars in his right hand and walks among the seven golden lampstands.*—Revelation 2:1

In Revelation 2:8, for the church in Smyrna, Jesus repeats his identity as the First and the Last, and as the one who died and came to life again.

> *These are the words of him who is the First and the Last, who died and came to life again.*—Revelation 2:8

In Revelation 2:12, Jesus has the words of a double-edged sword. In Revelation 2:18-19, in speaking to the church in Pergamum as the second person in the Trinity, Jesus wields the authority that comes with the sharp, double-edged sword. The sharpness emphasizes the complete and quick blow that can come from his judgment. The double-edged sword is a reminder that Jesus has the authority to both bless and to curse, to reward and to punish.

> *These are the words of him who has the sharp, double-edged sword.*
> —Revelation 2:12

> *Son of God, whose eyes are like blazing fire and whose feet are like burnished bronze. I know your deeds, your love and faith, your service and perseverance*—Revelation 2:18-19

In Revelation 2:27, Jesus, the Son, claims his authority from God the Father, and He can give authority to the victorious one to rule over the nations on earth.

I have received authority from my Father.—Revelation 2:27

Reflection

1. Describe your "first love" of God or of Jesus. Do you feel the same way now?

2. When have I felt victorious in my spiritual life? When have I felt defeated? Why?

3. What would it be like to eat from the tree of life in the paradise of God, as Adam and Eve did in the Garden?

4. Have I experienced extraordinary suffering? How can I still feel "rich" in the midst of poverty or great need?

5. Am I willing and prepared to die for the sake of Jesus Christ and the gospel? Why or why not? How can I be more prepared to make that sacrifice, if necessary?

6. When have I had to practice "patient endurance"? What did I do to help myself or others through difficult circumstances? In temporary or permanent conditions?

7. If God searched my heart at this very minute, what would he discover? Would I be satisfied with his findings?

8. When have I been tempted to slide toward Satan's "deeper truths" or false practices and prophecies? How do I safeguard against this in the future?

Chapter Three

Revelation 3

REVELATION 3:1-6 MESSAGE TO THE CHURCH IN SARDIS

Jesus refutes their reputation of being alive (spiritually) by proclaiming that they are dead, or they exhibit little evidence of a spiritual life. Their actions do not meet God's requirements. He admonishes them to go back to what they first heard and believed and to hold to it firmly. If not, Jesus will come to the unrepentant as unexpectedly as a thief. For the victorious, Jesus promises never to erase their names from the Book of Life and will announce before God and his angels that they are his. Again, Jesus shows an intimacy with those who maintain their belief in him.

REVELATION 3:7-13 MESSAGE TO THE CHURCH IN PHILADELPHIA

Jesus says that he knows all the things they do, and he has opened a door for them that no one can close. Jesus recognizes that they have little strength, but they obeyed his word and did not deny him. Because of their perseverance, Jesus makes several awesome promises to his faithful of Philadelphia:

(1) Jesus promises the victorious that he will protect them from the great time of testing.

> *The one who is **victorious** will, like them, be dressed in white. I will never blot out the name of that person from the book of life, but will acknowledge that name before my Father and his angels.*—Revelation 3:5-7

(2) Jesus promises to force those belonging to Satan to come and bow down at the feet of the Jesus followers. Even the Satanists will acknowledge that the Christians are the ones whom Jesus loves.

> *I will make those who are of the synagogue of **Satan**, who claim to be Jews though they are not, but are liars—I will make them come and fall down at your feet and acknowledge that I have loved you.*—Revelation 3:9

(3) Jesus promises that they will become pillars in the Temple of God, never to leave it.

(4) Jesus will write on them the name of God and give them citizenship in the city of God, the new Jerusalem.

(5) Jesus promises to write on them his new name.

The one who is ***victorious*** *I will make a pillar in the temple of my God. Never again will they leave it. I will write on them the name of my God and the name of the city of my God, the new Jerusalem, which is coming down out of heaven from my God; and I will also write on them my new name.* —Revelation 3:12

REVELATION 3:14-22 MESSAGE TO THE CHURCH OF LAODICEA

Jesus said to the church of Philadelphia and to the church of Laodicea, "I know all the things that you do." However, he follows this statement with rewards upon rewards for Philadelphia, but Jesus follows this statement to Laodicea by condemning them for being lukewarm, neither hot nor cold. Wishing that they were one or the other, Jesus warns that he will spit them out of his mouth because they think they are rich, but they are actually wretched, miserable, poor, blind, and naked. Jesus advises them to buy his gold that has been purified by fire, to buy his white garments to avoid shame, and to buy his ointment for their eyes for them to be able to see.

After his harsh words to the Laodiceans, Jesus tells them that he corrects and disciplines everyone he loves and admonishes them to be diligent and turn from their indifference.

Following this is one of the most quoted scriptures where Jesus extends to his faithful the opportunity for the intimacy of a shared meal as friends. Jesus promises the **victorious** that they will sit with him on his throne.

Here I am! I stand at the door and knock. If anyone hears my voice and opens the door, I will come in and eat with that person, and they with me. To the one who is ***victorious,*** *I will give the right to sit with me on my throne, just as I was* ***victorious*** *and sat down with my Father on his throne."*— Revelation 3:20-21

Thematically, Chapter 3 continues focusing on the authority of Jesus as the second Person in the Trinity. He reveals the nature and identity of God through his power as the Son of God.

To the church in Sardis, in Revelation 3:1, Jesus says that he is the holder of the seven spirits of God and the seven stars and knows all their deeds. The seven spirits are listed in Isaiah 11 as the Spirit of the Lord, Wisdom, Understanding, Counsel, Might, Knowledge, and the Fear of the Lord. The seven stars are presumed to be the seven angels or messengers or pastors to the seven churches.

> *A shoot will come up from the stump of Jesse; from his roots a Branch will bear fruit. 2 The Spirit of the Lord will rest on him – the Spirit of wisdom and of understanding, the Spirit of counsel and of might, the Spirit of knowledge and fear of the Lord – 3 and he will delight in the fear of the Lord.*—Isaiah 11:1-3

To the church in Philadelphia, in Revelation 3:7, Jesus calls himself holy and true. He is of the bloodline of David with all the authority of kingship. His authority is emphasized by the power to be the only one to open or shut the figurative doors of heaven and Hades. He is all knowing of the deeds of his people.

> *... him who is holy and true, who holds the key of David. What he opens no one can shut, and what he shuts no one can open. I know your deeds.*— Revelation 3:7

Jesus is our protector. He has the authority to protect us in times of trials.

> *Since you have kept my command to endure patiently, I will also keep you from the hour of trial that is going to come on the whole world to test the inhabitants of the earth.*—Revelation 3:10

Jesus has the knowledge of the name of God and of his new name. To have the personal name of God shows intimacy, connection, and shared attributes with God. Having a new name aligns with patterns in the New and Old Testament of people receiving a new name after a spiritual, Godly interaction or event or calling. From his humble birth to his transfiguration on the mountain to his ascension into heaven, Jesus has taken many forms of humanity and divinity. This new name signifies a magnified identity for Jesus upon God's final judgment.

> *I will write on them the name of my God and the name of the city of my God, the new Jerusalem, which is coming down out of heaven from my God; and I will also write on them my new name.*—Revelation 3:12

To the church in Laodicea, in Revelation 3:14, Jesus is the Amen, the embodiment of truth. He is faithful and a true witness of everything that has taken place or that will take place. He rules all of God's creation. All of the descriptors signify an authoritative, powerful Jesus Christ. Not only is Jesus the last say, he has the last say and knows all of our deeds. There is nothing gentle or timid about this Jesus.

> *The Amen, the faithful and true witness, the ruler of God's creation. I know your deeds.*—Revelation 3:14-15

Reflection

1. Are there times when I have felt "spiritually dead"? During those times, what can I do to become "spiritually alive" again?

2. How can I prevent myself from sliding into a spiritually dead state of being?

3. When I come into contact with people who worship Satan or who deny God and Jesus, how do I treat them and how do I witness to them?

4. How have I shown perseverance in my faith in Jesus, especially when I was not strong?

5. What door has Jesus opened for me that will never close?

6. Am I "on fire" for Jesus, or am I "lukewarm" in my passion for following Jesus? When have I felt or acted indifferently in response to the Gospel message?

7. Have I thought that I was rich, but I am actually wretched, miserable, poor, or blind? What should I do to find clarity about my spiritual condition?

8. Do I feel close enough to Jesus to invite him into my home to eat a meal with me? What would we eat? What would we talk about?

Chapter Four

Revelation 4

REVELATION 4: WORSHIP IN HEAVEN

This chapter highlights the praise and worship to God the Father, Son, and Holy Spirit, especially more of the identity and nature of the Holy Spirit. John was invited to get a glimpse of heaven and those sitting on and around the throne. Twenty-four elders were clothed in white with gold crowns, and in front of the throne were seven torches with burning flames: the sevenfold Spirit of God.

Isaiah 11 lists seven characteristics of spirits of God: (1) the Spirit of the Lord; (2) the Spirit of Wisdom; (3) the Spirit of Understanding; (4) the Spirit of Counsel; (5) the Spirit of Strength; (6) the Spirit of Knowledge; and (7) the Spirit of the Fear of the Lord.

> *A shoot will come up from the stump of Jesse;*
> *And his roots a Branch will bear fruit;*
> *The Spirit of the Lord will rest on him–*
> *The Spirit of wisdom and of understanding,*
> *the Spirit of counsel and of might,*
> *the Spirit of the knowledge and fear of the Lord–*
> *and he will delight in the fear of the Lord.*—Isaiah 11:1-3

The sevenfold Spirit of God is mentioned again in Revelation 5:6 in a description of Jesus:

> *Then I saw a Lamb, looking as if it had been slain, standing at the center of the throne, encircled by the four living creatures and the elders. The Lamb had seven horns and seven eyes, which are the seven spirits of God sent out into all the earth.*—Revelation 5:6

Revelation 4:6-11 is a description of four living beings, each looking like different animals: a lion, an ox, a human face, and an eagle in flight. These match the four beings in Ezekiel's vision (Ezekiel 1) of multiple eyes, multiple wings, and leading worship before the throne of God:

> *Their faces looked like this: Each of the four had the face of a human being, and on the right side each had the face of a lion, and on the left the face of an ox; each also had the face of an eagle.* —Ezekiel 1:10

In Revelation 4:9-11, whenever the four beings give glory to the one on the throne, the 24 elders do the same. The response to their worship also resonates in Ezekiel's vision.

> *Wherever the spirit would go, they would go, and the wheels would rise along with them, because the spirit of the living creatures was in the wheels. When the creatures moved, they also moved; when the creatures stood still, they also stood still; and when the creatures rose from the ground, the wheels rose along with them, because the spirit of the living creatures was in the wheels.* —Ezekiel 1:20-21

Do these four beings represent the categories of God's creations: humans, wild beasts, domesticated beasts, and birds? Do the four living creatures represent the evangelists Matthew, Mark, Luke, and John? Wikipedia® suggests, "The most common interpretation, first laid out by Victorinus and adopted by Jerome, St Gregory, and the Book of Kells, is that the man is Matthew, the lion Mark, the ox Luke, and the eagle John. The creatures of the tetramorph, just like the four gospels of the Evangelists, represent four facets of Christ." Whether the four beings represent all of God's creations or all facets of Christ in the vision of Ezekiel and the Revelation to John, these beings lead the worship around the throne. The four beings lead worship with:

> *"Holy, holy, holy*
> *Is the Lord God Almighty,*
> *Who was, and is, and is to come."*—Revelation 4:8b

Then the 24 elders follow by falling down and laying their crowns before the throne saying,

> *"You are worthy, our Lord and God,*
> *to receive glory and honor and power,*
> *for you created all things,*
> *and by your will they were created*
> *and have their being."* —Revelation 4:11

I do not profess to be an accomplished theologian, but I do wonder why John would not have recognized himself as being the eagle in flight. Is it possible that people put significance into these symbols beyond what is explained in Scriptures? Taking into account the swell of worship in Revelation 5, from the living beings, elders, angels, and every creature in heaven and on earth and under the earth, I could more easily accept the interpretation of the four beings as representative of all of God's creations.

Regarding the theme of God's nature and identity, God the Father is featured in Revelation Chapter 4. The sovereign God sits on the throne and lives forever. He is worthy to receive glory, honor and power. God created all things by his will. All living beings exist because of God, and their continuous praise refers to God, who is holy, mighty, and eternal.

> *Each of the four living creatures had six wings and was covered with eyes all around, even under its wings. Day and night they never stop saying:: "'**Holy, holy, holy** is the **Lord God Almighty**,' **who was, and is, and is to come.**"*—Revelation 4:8

> *Whenever the living creatures give glory, honor and thanks to **him who sits on the throne and who lives for ever and ever**, the twenty-four elders fall down before **him who sits on the throne** and worship **him who lives for ever and ever**. They lay their crowns before the throne and say:*

> *"You are **worthy, our Lord** and God,*
> *to receive glory and honor and power,*
> *for **you created all things,***
> ***and by your will they were created***
> *and have their being."* — Revelation 4:9-11

Reflection

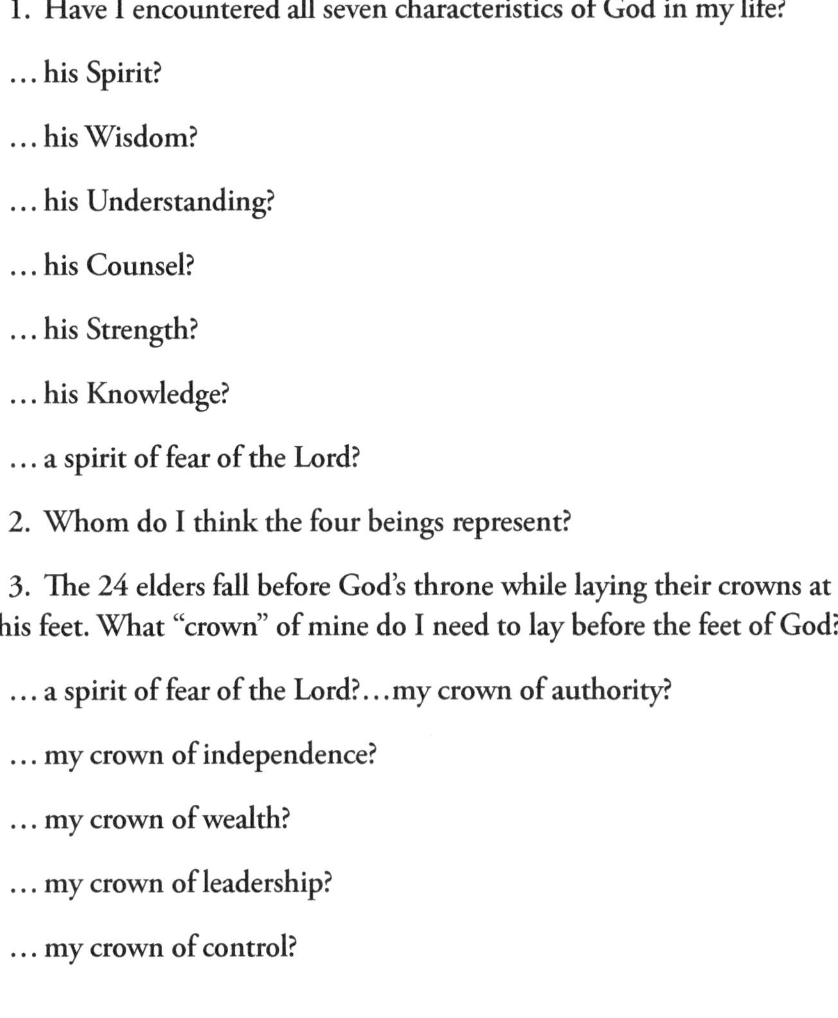

1. Have I encountered all seven characteristics of God in my life?

…his Spirit?

…his Wisdom?

…his Understanding?

…his Counsel?

…his Strength?

…his Knowledge?

…a spirit of fear of the Lord?

2. Whom do I think the four beings represent?

3. The 24 elders fall before God's throne while laying their crowns at his feet. What "crown" of mine do I need to lay before the feet of God?

…a spirit of fear of the Lord?…my crown of authority?

…my crown of independence?

…my crown of wealth?

…my crown of leadership?

…my crown of control?

Chapter Five

Revelation 5

REVELATION 5: THE LAMB OPENS THE SCROLL

The theme of praise continues in Chapter 5, not just repeated choruses of praise, but new songs sung by the living beings and elders, as well as millions of angels joining in a mighty chorus. It is Jesus, the mighty Lamb of God, the lion of the tribe of Judah, and the heir to David's throne. Jesus is the center of praise with his Father God.

After bemoaning the fact that no one in heaven or on earth or under the earth was able to open the scroll, one of the 24 elders explained to John that the only one worthy was the "Lion of the tribe of Judah, the heir to David's throne". Then the Lamb appeared as if slaughtered but standing among the beings and elders. The Lamb, Jesus, had seven horns and seven eyes, representing the sevenfold Spirit of God that is sent out into every part of the earth.

> *But no one in heaven or on earth or under the earth could open the scroll or even look inside it. I wept and wept because no one was found who was worthy to open the scroll or look inside. Then one of the elders said to me, "Do not weep! See, the Lion of the tribe of Judah, the Root of David, has triumphed. He is able to open the scroll and its seven seals."* —Revelation 5:3

With gold bowls filled with incense representing the prayers of God's people, the beings and elders fall down before the Lamb as he opens the scroll. They sing a new song:

> *You are worthy to take the scroll*
> *and to open its seals,*
> *because you were slain,*
> *and with your blood you purchased for God*
> *persons from every tribe and language and people and nation.*
> *You have made them to be a kingdom and priests to serve our God,*
> *and they will reign on the earth."*—Revelation 5:9-10

Included in this new song is a recurring reference to Jesus' blood being shed for people from all tribes and languages and people and nations made to be a kingdom and priests to serve God.

The angels joined in worship, thousand and millions in a mighty chorus in Revelation 5:12.

> *"Worthy is the Lamb, who was slain,*
> *to receive power and wealth and wisdom and strength*
> *and honor and glory and praise!"*—Revelation 5:12

The Revelation captures the images of continuous praise to God in heaven by all of creation, not just human beings, but all living beings, elders, angels, and "every creature in heaven and on earth and under the earth and on the sea, and all that is in them":

> *Then I heard every creature in heaven and on earth and under the earth and on the sea, and all that is in them, saying:*
> *"To him who sits on the throne and to the Lamb*
> *be praise and honor and glory and power,*
> *for ever and ever!"*—Revelation 5:13

One can just imagine the worship swelling in volume and numbers of those singing praise to God! All of creation everywhere in all forms in, on, and under the earth sing praise to God. This swelling of praise to God from all his creations is concluded with the four living beings saying, "Amen!" at which point the 24 elders fall down before the Lamb, all worshiping Him continually and eternally.

In the gospel of Luke, chapter 19, Jesus entered Jerusalem as people were spreading their cloaks on the ground before him, riding on a colt. When the Pharisees rebuked them, Jesus said that if they did not praise him, even the rocks would cry out.

> *When he came near the place where the road goes down the Mount of Olives, the whole crowd of disciples began joyfully to praise God in loud voices for all the miracles they had seen:*
>
> *"Blessed is the king who comes in the name of the Lord!"*
>
> *"Peace in heaven and glory in the highest!"*
>
> *Some of the Pharisees in the crowd said to Jesus, "Teacher, rebuke your disciples!"*
>
> *"I tell you," he replied, "if they keep quiet, the stones will cry out."* —Luke 19:37-40

The image of rocks crying out is not so incredible when reading the praises to God from every creature described in Revelation 5:13. If we ever run out of words to praise God, we can emulate the words of the multitudes around God's throne. Reading, speaking, and singing the words of praise in Revelation is good practice.

> *Let everything that has breath praise the Lord. Praise the Lord.*—Psalm 150:6

Regarding the theme of the nature and identity of God in the Trinity, Chapter 5 highlights the strong relationship between Father God and Son Jesus. God the Father, is seated on his throne in heaven while Son Jesus is called as the only one worthy to open the scroll with writing on both sides and sealed with seven seals. Several times in this chapter, God, the Father, is seated on his throne receiving the Spirit of praise while the crescendo of praise extends to His Son, Jesus!

> *Then I saw in the right hand of* ***him who sat on the throne*** *a scroll with writing on both sides and sealed with seven seals.*—Revelation 5:1

> *He went and took the scroll from the right hand of* ***him who sat on the throne.***—Revelation 5:7

> *"To* ***him who sits on the throne*** *and to the Lamb*
> *be praise and honor and glory and power,*
> *for ever and ever!"*—Revelation 5:13

As the only one worthy of opening the scroll, Jesus is identified as the Lion of the tribe of Judah, which puts him in the family bloodline of Judah himself, King David, King Solomon, and Jesus. He is the victor in his triumph, and his triumph happens when He acts of the Lamb of God, who takes away the sin of the world by his blood sacrifice on the cross. Jesus is seen as the Lamb who was slain at the center of God's throne. This image would be familiar to John because he calls Jesus the Lamb of God as he sees Jesus approaching him before baptizing him in the Jordan River.

> *The next day John saw Jesus coming toward him and said, "Look, the Lamb of God, who takes away the sin of the world!* — John 1:29

> *See, the Lion of the tribe of Judah, the Root of David, has triumphed.*—Revelation 5:5

> *Then I saw a Lamb, looking as if it had been slain, standing at the center of the throne, encircled by the four living creatures and the elders. The Lamb had seven horns and seven eyes, which are the seven spirits of God sent out into all the earth.*—Revelation 5:6

Jesus is worthy; his shed blood purchased persons from every group of people in the world; and he made them part of his kingdom to serve as priest for God.

> *And they sang a new song, saying:*
> *"You are worthy to take the scroll*
> *and to open its seals,*
> *because you were slain,*
> *and with your blood you purchased for God*
> *persons from every tribe and language and people and nation.*
> *You have made them to be a kingdom and priests to serve our God,*
> *and they will reign on the earth."*—Revelation 5:9-10

The praise continues for Jesus around the throne in heaven, first by thousands and thousands of angels, then all living creatures praising Jesus and the Lord God.

> *In a loud voice they were says*
> *"Worthy is the Lamb, who was slain,*
> *to receive power and wealth and wisdom and strength*
> *and honor and glory and praise!"*—Revelation 5:12

The continuous outpouring of praise now to the Father and Son in the Spirit strengthens their unity and identity as the One God in Three Persons. The whole family of God worships the Triune Family of God over and over in magnanimous words of harmonious, melodic praise! Who wouldn't want to join the living in heaven for this continuous worship service?

Reflection

1. What does my song of praise sound like? What words would I use to praise God?

2. How comfortable am I to embrace the idea of every tribe and language and people and nation bowing before the throne of God? Does this include being comfortable with every person, even those close to me or in my family, bowing before the throne of God with me?

3. Imagine hearing the swelling of praise in great volume. What does that mean to me in relation to hearing praise sung in Christian groups and events?

4. In 5:13 when I join with "every creature in heaven and on earth and under the earth and on the sea, and all that is in them" in giving praise to God, am I ready to join every creature on earth and in the sea? How does this verse change my view of who goes to heaven and who praises God.

CHAPTER SIX

Revelation 6

REVELATION 6: THE LAMB BREAKS THE FIRST SIX SEALS

The Lamb broke the first four seals to reveal four horses: (1) a white horse, carrying a rider with a bow and a crown as he rode out to win many battles; (2) a red horse, carrying a rider with a mighty sword and authority to take peace from the earth, where there was war and slaughter everywhere; (3) a black horse, carrying a rider holding a pair of scales indicative of the imbalance of the economy; and (4) a pale green horse, carrying a rider named "Death" and his companion named the "Grave", who were given authority over one quarter of the earth to kill with the sword and by famine, disease and wild animals.

The Lamb broke the fifth seal to reveal an altar over the souls of all who had been martyred for the word of God and their testimony. When they asked how long before the Lord would bring judgment, they were given white robes and told to rest a little longer until the full number of their brother and sister martyrs would join them.

The Lamb broke the sixth seal to reveal a great earthquake when the sun became dark and the moon red as blood. The stars fell to earth from the sky with all of the mountains and islands moved from their places.

Everyone, from kings to slaves, hid in caves and among the rocks of the mountains, where they cried to the mountains and rocks, "Fall on us and hide us from the face of the one who sits on the throne and from the wrath of the Lamb. For the great day of their wrath has come, and who is able to survive?"

From these six seals, the prophecy shows the earth at war, the Lamb of Life against Death and the Grave. The number of martyrs will increase, leaving the people of God wondering if they will survive. At every point in history, there has been war waged in some part of the earth. Throughout history, people have been martyred for their faith, and the persecution is still happening today. Will we be able to survive it all? Chapter Seven answers the question: "Yes!"

Regarding the theme of the nature and identity of God in Revelation, God the Father has sovereignty over heaven and earth while Jesus the Son demonstrates this sovereignty by victoriously carrying out the wrath of God against the evils of his enemies. God remains seated on his throne as Jesus (at times his angels) inflict his wrath upon the earth. Not only God, but Jesus poised as the Lamb, who has the power to inflict wrath on the unjust of the earth.

In Revelation 6:2, as the first of the seven seals is broken by the Lamb, John sees the image of Jesus wearing a crown and riding a white horse. He is already seen as being victorious in the battle against the enemy.

> *I looked, and there before me was a white horse! Its rider held a bow, and he was given a crown, and he rode out as a conqueror bent on conquest.* —Revelation 6:2

God is Sovereign, holy and true. He has the supreme and ultimate power. He is holy and true with all intentions and purposes toward what is good for all. God is the one who has the power to judge all on earth and to avenge the blood of the martyrs, those slain because of the word of God and their testimony.

> *When he opened the fifth seal, I saw under the altar the souls of those who had been slain because of the word of God and the testimony they had maintained. 10 They called out in a loud voice, "How long,* ***Sovereign Lord, holy and true,*** *until* ***you judge*** *the inhabitants of the earth and* ***avenge*** *our blood?"*—Revelation 6:9-10

> *They called to the mountains and the rocks, "Fall on us and hide us from the face of him who sits on the throne and from the wrath of the Lamb!* —Revelation 6:9-1

History and tradition recount that John was the only one of Jesus' twelve disciples to escape death by martyrdom. He most probably was already aware that his beloved friends and relatives were being slain because of the word of God and their testimony. However, these two tenets of purpose for John would bring him into unity of the cause for Christ, as well as unity in the danger of becoming a martyr by being a Christ follower. John must have known the potential dangers of his calling, but he dutifully listened, took note, and communicated every word of his Revelation.

Reflection

1. What martyrs do I know from biblical history?

2. What martyrs do I know from modern history?

3. Am I ready to be a martyr, should the time come to give my life for the gospel of Jesus Christ?

4. What types of persecution are happening in my life? What can I do about it?

5. There always seems to be war somewhere in the world. Which ones appear to be motivated by spiritual or religious differences?

CHAPTER SEVEN

Revelation 7

REVELATION 7: GOD'S PEOPLE WILL BE PRESERVED

Four angels held back the four winds of destruction to the earth and sea until a fifth angel came carrying the seal of the living God to be placed on the foreheads of his servants. 144,000 people representing all twelve tribes of Israel received the seal in equal numbers: 12,000. Following this, a vast crowd from every nation, tribe, people, and language stood before the throne and the Lamb, shouting praises with palm branches with a mighty roar. Described by John as "too great to count", the crowd shouts:

> *"Salvation belongs to our God who sits on the throne, and to the Lamb!"*
> —Revelation 7:10

Then the angels and elders and four living beings worship God in song:

> *"Amen! Blessing and glory and wisdom,*
> *Thanksgiving and honor and power and might,*
> *Be to our God forever and ever.*
> *Amen."*—Revelation 7:12

This scene is reminiscent of Jesus' entry into Jerusalem as he rides a donkey while followers hail him with waving palm branches.

> *The next day a great multitude that had come to the feast, when they heard that Jesus was coming to Jerusalem, 13 took branches of palm trees and went out to meet Him, and cried out:*
>
> *"Hosanna! 'Blessed is He who comes in the name of the Lord!'*
> *The King of Israel!"*
>
> *Then Jesus, when He had found a young donkey, sat on it; as it is written:*
> *"Fear not, daughter of Zion;*
> *Behold, your King is coming,*
> *Sitting on a donkey's colt."*—John 12:12-15

> *He was fulfilling the prophecy in Zechariah:*
> *"Rejoice greatly, O daughter of Zion!*
> *Shout, O daughter of Jerusalem!*
> *Behold, your King is coming to you;*
>
> *He is just and having salvation,*
> *Lowly and riding on a donkey,"* —Revelation 5:12

The Revelation captures the images of continuous praise to God in heaven by all of creation, not just human beings, but all living beings, elders, angels, and "every creature in heaven and on earth and under the earth and on the sea, and all that is in them":

> *Then I heard every creature in heaven and on earth and under the earth and on the sea, and all that is in them, saying:*
>
> *"To him who sits on the throne and to the Lamb*
> *be praise and honor and glory and power,*
> *for ever and ever!""* — Revelation 5:13

By his actions as he rode into Jerusalem, Jesus publicly acknowledged himself as a king of Israel, just not the kind of king that the people were expecting. The people soon turned on him and shouted for him to be crucified. In the Revelation, when people waved palm branches, this time they shouted before the throne of God and praised the Lamb, Jesus, for saving them from Death and the Grave. What a difference three days made as Jesus rose from the dead and proved that he is who he said he is.

I think about the palm wavers in Jerusalem, and wonder what they may have thought after Jesus was sentenced to death on a cross. They once waved him on as king; then they waved him to his death. How awesome in this prophecy to John that the faithful were able to wave palm branches before Jesus in heaven.

Chapter 7:14 describes the faithful waving palms before the throne as the ones who died in the great tribulation. They had endured great suffering and had washed their robes in the blood of the Lamb and made them white. The Lamb on the throne continues to be their Shepherd.

> *He will lead them to springs of life-giving water. And God will wipe every tear from their eyes.* — Revelation 7:17

The theme of the identity and nature of God is extended in Chapter 7 to show us a "living God" who possesses a range of Godly emotions from wrath to compassion. We can relate to this personal God, whom we both fear and love. We fear him for his power to punish the unrepentant souls, and we love him for his endless capacity to love us and to save us from ourselves.

In Revelation 7:2, the description of God being "the living" God is significant because the God of the Revelation is alive, unlike the other gods and idols of the ages.

> *Then I saw another angel coming up from the east, having the seal of **the living God.***—Revelation 7:2

God sits on the throne in heaven, and he has the power to save, as does Jesus, the Lamb of God.

> *And they cried out in a loud voice:*
> ***"Salvation belongs to our God,***
> ***who sits on the throne,***
> *and to the Lamb."*— Revelation 7:10

Enter an extension of God's hands: his angels, messengers who obey God and give him praise continually while describing and affirming his nature. God is wise, honorable, powerful, strong, and eternally worthy of praise and glory, from beginning to end, from Amen to Amen!

> ***"Amen!***
> ***Praise and glory***
> ***and wisdom and thanks and honor***
> ***and power and strength***
> ***be to our God** for ever and ever.*
> *Amen!"*—Revelation 7:12

The powerful God capable of wreaking havoc on his enemies is also capable of showing love, gentleness, mercy, and compassion to His own. In chapter 7, John writes of the gentle, consoling, saving nature of God: the God who leads his people to life-giving water and wipes every tear from their eyes.

This image of both a wrathful but compassionate God is also reflected in the New Testament images of Jesus, the Son of God. Like Father, like Son, Jesus righteously flipped over the tables of the disrespectful merchants in His Father's temple, and Jesus showed compassion offering rest to the weary.

> *Jesus entered the temple courts and drove out all who were buying and selling there. He overturned the tables of the money changers and the benches of those selling doves.*—Matthew 21:12

> *"Come to me, all you who are weary and burdened, and I will give you rest. Take my yoke upon you and learn from me, for I am gentle and humble in heart, and you will find rest for your souls. 30 For my yoke is easy and my burden is light."*—Matthew 11:28-29

The rest that Jesus promises is reflected in John's Revelation as the redeemed from the great tribulation serve God before the throne in his temple. They have the total protection and provision of God. In heaven, there is no hunger, thirst, discomfort of the elements, or sadness. As the Lamb of God, Jesus is seated at the center of the throne and acts as their shepherd.

Therefore,
*"they are before the **throne of God***
*and serve him day and night **in his temple;***
*and **he who sits on the throne***
will shelter them with his presence.

'Never again will they hunger;
never again will they thirst.
The sun will not beat down on them,'
nor any scorching heat.

For the Lamb at the center of the throne
will be their shepherd;
'he will lead them to springs of living water.'
*'And **God will wipe away every tear** from their eyes.'"*
—Revelation 7:15-17

Reflection

1. **What tears of mine will God wipe from my eyes?**

2. **Have I endured great suffering? How has God helped me through it?**

3. **Do I believe that Jesus really is who he says he is? Do I have any doubts as to his divinity and role as the Son of God? What can I do about my doubts or fears about God and my relationship with him?**

CHAPTER EIGHT

Revelation 8

REVELATION 8: THE LAMB BREAKS THE SEVENTH SEAL

Up to this point, we have heard shouts of praise and loud voices. Dramatically, when the Lamb broke the seventh seal of the scroll, there was total silence in heaven for about half an hour. Quietly, another angel mixes incense with the prayers of God's people as the smoke ascends to God. In the quiet, God hears our prayers before his judgment of the earth begins.

After the prayers were delivered to God, the angel filled the incense burner with fire from the altar and threw it to earth causing a terrible earthquake. Along with thunder and lightning came the mighty trumpet blasts of the seven angels--all with disastrous results:

- The first angel's blast came with hail and fire mixed with blood and one third of the earth was set on fire.
- The second angel's blast resulted in a great mountain of fire thrown into the sea with one third of the sea turned to blood, one third of sea creatures dead, and one third of all ships destroyed.
- The third angel's blast came with a great star falling from the sky, burning like a torch with one third of the rivers and springs turning bitter. Many people died from drinking the bitter water.
- The fourth angel's blast caused one third of the sun and the moon and stars to become dark.

Readers of this chapter might have a range of emotional responses. Some may feel a sense of fear that death and destruction is near. Others may feel numb and desensitized from the daily barrage of bad news around the world: wars, famine, wildfires, floods, plagues, and economic disasters. Rather than dreading or dismissing this part of the prophecy, we should focus on the precious attention that God gives to his people and their needs. Heaven was silenced for half an hour for the prayers of God's people to ascend to his altar. If heaven was silenced, then that must mean that God put a hold on the shouts of continual praise to him so that he could receive our prayers with no other distractions, even good ones. Whether our prayers were spoken, unspoken, written, sung, strummed, or drummed, this silence commanded for a half an hour indicated that our prayers must be a very special form of praise to God. Our prayers were mixed with incense for that holy fragrance to rise to God's altar and to please his senses. This 30-minute silence was the literal "calm before the storm" of judgment, and it was a personal notice of God's people and his relationship with them. He sees, hears, and knows our needs.

A single eagle then announced terror ahead with the blast of the last three angels' trumpets. The terror would come to all who belong to this world. That terror was for those who do not belong to Jesus, to God.

God seems to be giving incremental warnings to the people of this world, starting with one third of all living things, but the eagle's cry indicates that the terror is reserved for those who do not belong to the Lamb, to Jesus. The incremental warnings reflect the incredible patience that God has for his lost people. We are given an order of events but not specific time passages between these trumpet blasts and the terrors to come. The only time listed was the half an hour of silence. The unspecified time related to the angels' blasts bringing destruction could be "soon" or a thousand years or anything more or less. Over and over in the history of his people, God has waited for repentance, has given second and third chances, and has spoken his intentions clearly to all. He wants that none should perish, and he has been willing to wait for us to use our free will to believe in his Son, Jesus.

> *For God so loved the world that He gave His only begotten Son, that whoever believes in Him should not perish but have everlasting life.*
> —John 3:16

Regardless of the time or form of judgment, the prophecy makes clear that our best response to all of this is to decide right now that we believe in God's Son and receive the love that God has for us all.

Reflection

1. When I think about God receiving my prayers with incense rising before him at his throne, what specific prayers do I want to add to the golden incense burner?

2. Have I thought about the fact that God hears every prayer from the past, present, or future?

3. How special am I that God would suspend praise around his throne to receive my prayers and all the prayers of the faithful?

4. Do I truly believe in God's Son? Have I received the love of God in all of its fullness? Am I willing to share his love with others?

CHAPTER NINE

Revelation 9

REVELATION 9: THE FIFTH AND SIXTH TRUMPETS BRING THE FIRST & SECOND TERRORS

When the fifth angel blew his trumpet, a star had fallen to earth and was given the key to the bottomless pit. When the star opened the Abyss, smoke poured out like the smoke from a huge furnace, and the sunlight and air turned dark from the smoke. As previously stated, the stars are symbolic of angels, so this fallen star with keys to the pit must refer to Satan, who was the angel who fell from heaven and was cast to earth. Armored locusts looking like horses prepared for battle emerged from the smoke and tortured those people who did not have the seal of God on their foreheads. Verse 11 identifies their king as the angel from the bottomless pit named Abaddon (in Hebrew) or Apollyon (in Greek), also known as the Destroyer or Wormwood. As the first terror passed, two more were promised.

When the sixth angel blew his trumpet, a voice from the presence of God told the angel to release the four angels who were bound at the great Euphrates River. The four angels with an army of 200 million mounted troops killed one third of all the people on earth from three plagues: fire, smoke, and burning sulfur. The horses had heads like lions with fire and smoke billowing from their mouths. Amazingly, the people who survived the plagues still refused to repent of their demon worship, murders, witchcraft, sexual immorality, or their thefts. How many warnings will it take for people to turn to God before the final judgment? Apparently, and sadly, some never will.

Reflection

1. **Why do people refuse to repent, even when they see the consequences of their sins?**

2. **Do I need to repent from any form of demon worship, witchcraft, murder, sexual immorality or theft? In what way?**

3. **Demon worship and witchcraft: Do I need to repent of demon worship because of my participation in seances, fortune telling, palm reading, reading literature focused on demons, video games that**

glorify demons, Halloween activities that encourage the occult, etc.?

- Murder: Do I need to repent from having or paying for an abortion? Do I support abortion or work in a medical facility that aborts babies? Do I support any political causes that promote violence, wars, genocide, etc.? Do I need to repent for not praying about (maybe even caring about) senseless acts of murder?

- Sexual immorality: Do I need to repent from watching movies or television shows that encourage lust, adultery, sexual perversions? Do I need to repent from my participation in acts of sexual impurity, adultery, or lust?

- Theft: Do I need to repent from stealing things? Do I need to repent from stealing time from my place of employment by doing non-related activities during work time? Do I need to repent from cheating on my taxes or short-changing my tithes and offerings? Do I need to repent from "stealing someone's youth" by mistreatment or abuse of children? Do I need to repent from stealing time from others in family relationships through alienation?

4. What have been peoples' responses to plagues in modern times (like COVID, HIV, influenza? Do they associate plagues with the wrath of God?

5. Do I believe that Satan, or the devil, is real? Why or why not?

Chapter Ten

Revelation 10

REVELATION 10: THE ANGEL AND THE SMALL SCROLL

John describes another mighty angel coming from heaven with a rainbow over his head, face like the sun, and feet like pillars of fire. He had his right foot on the sea and his left foot on the land. With a great shout like the roar of a lion, the seven thunders answered, but John was not permitted to write their words down. The angel swore an oath to the Creator and said that there would be no more delay. John was directed to take the open scroll and eat it, and when he did, the scroll tasted sweet as honey in his mouth but soured in his stomach.

> *Then he was told, "You must prophesy again about many peoples, nations, languages, and kings."*—Revelation 10:11

Similar to John, the prophet Ezekiel had a vision in which God called him "son of man" and directed him to eat a scroll that tasted sweet as honey.

> *And he said to me, "Son of man, eat what is before you, eat this scroll; then go and speak to the people of Israel." So I opened my mouth, and he gave me the scroll to eat.*
>
> *Then he said to me, "Son of man, eat this scroll I am giving you and fill your stomach with it." So I ate it, and it tasted as sweet as honey in my mouth.*—Ezekiel 3:1-3

The words of the Lord tasted sweet in his mouth, but then God told Ezekiel that the people of Israel will be hard hearted and obstinate, refusing to believe his message to them. How frustrating to receive a sweet message from God and then to have such difficulty delivering the message to his people.

> *But the people of Israel are not willing to listen to you because they are not willing to listen to me, for all the Israelites are hardened and obstinate. But I will make you as unyielding and hardened as they are. I will make your forehead like the hardest stone, harder than flint. Do not be afraid of them or terrified by them, though they are a rebellious people.*—Ezekiel 3:7-9

Then Ezekiel went away in bitterness and anger to deliver God's message. This feeling could also be described as feeling a sourness in his stomach, just as John felt in Revelation, upon learning that not all people would accept his message.

> *The Spirit then lifted me up and took me away, and I went in bitterness and in the anger of my spirit, with the strong hand of the Lord on me. I came to the exiles who lived at Tel Aviv near the Kebar River. And there, where they were living, I sat among them for seven days—deeply distressed.*
> —Ezekiel 3:14-15

Now that would give Ezekiel one sour stomach, maybe even intestinal distress: to be sitting for seven days among people who don't want to hear what he has to say directly from God.

For both the prophet Ezekiel and the prophet John in Revelation, they consumed the words of God (via the scrolls) with the same delight in which we would consume a sweet delicacy made with honey. However, when they learned that unrepentant people would have difficulty "digesting" their sweet words of God, their stomachs felt sour from the challenge ahead of them.

Have you ever eaten a food and then realized that you are intolerant of something in the food? What tasted great going down gives you a feeling in your stomach of impending doom. That must have been how Ezekiel and John felt in their spirits, or stomachs, when they realized that delivering God's messages to his people is not as sweet as it first seems.

God's order for John to repeat the prophecy about the many peoples, nations, languages, and kings further emphasizes that all are to receive the prophecy and that the message of salvation and God's judgment is meant for everyone, not just the people of Israel. In Ezekiel's case, the prophecy was meant for the people of Israel, who were already familiar with the language. In John's case, he would be repeating the prophecy to people of many languages. To Ezekiel, God said that people of other nations would be more accepting of his message. That may have been encouraging to John.

> *You are not being sent to a people of obscure speech and strange language, but to the people of Israel—not to many peoples of obscure speech and strange language, whose words you cannot understand. Surely if I had sent you to them, they would have listened to you.*
> —Ezekiel 3:5-6

Reflection

1. How is the gospel message being spread to all peoples, nations, and languages today? Do I have a responsibility in spreading the Gospel to others? If so, how?

2. What is the significance of the rainbow over the head of the mighty angel?

3. Why was John not permitted to write the words of the seven thunders, who answered the mighty angel from heaven?

Chapter Eleven

Revelation 11

REVELATION 11: THE TWO WITNESSES

In this chapter, John is told that God will appoint two witnesses who will prophesy and who have the power to shut up the heavens so that it would not rain while they are prophesying. They have power to change the elements of the earth and to strike the earth with plagues.

> *And I will appoint my two witnesses, and they will prophesy for 1,260 days, clothed in sackcloth." They are "the two olive trees" and the two lampstands, and "they stand before the Lord of the earth." If anyone tries to harm them, fire comes from their mouths and devours their enemies. This is how anyone who wants to harm them must die. They have power to shut up the heavens so that it will not rain during the time they are prophesying; and they have power to turn the waters into blood and to strike the earth with every kind of plague as often as they want."*—Revelation 11:3-6

In Revelation 11:3-6, two prophets are clothed in burlap and prophesied for 42 months with protection from God. They have the power to shut the sky so that no rain would fall for as long as they prophesied. This is the exact number of months that Elijah prayed for Israel's rain to stop, and then he prayed for it to rain again immediately.

> *Elijah was a man with a nature like ours, and he prayed earnestly that it would not rain; and it did not rain on the land for three years and six months. And he prayed again, and the heaven gave rain, and the earth produced its fruit.*—James 5:17-18

If the reference is Elijah, then who is the second prophet? Presumably, the second prophet could be Moses, since Revelation 11:6 continues to describe the prophets' power to "turn the rivers and oceans into blood, and to strike the earth with every kind of plague as often as they wish." Moses lays claims to the most plagues in the Bible. God allowed the rain to stop and start again through the prayers of Elijah, and God ordained the 10 plagues of Egypt through Moses. Also, Peter, James, and John see Moses with Elijah with Jesus at his transfiguration on the mountain. John recognizing Moses, Elijah, and Jesus in their transfigured states in Revelation makes sense.

Moses and Elijah are also connected by the location where they left the earth. Both the burial site of Moses and the place where Elijah ascended to heaven in a chariot are purportedly near Mt. Nebo. Verse 8 refers to Sodom and Egypt as figurative names for Jerusalem, where Jesus was crucified, so again, the three figures are associated together in this chapter.

When the prophets completed their testimony, the beast was to come from the bottomless pit and kill them, but after three and a half days, God breathed life into them, and they stood up. Then they are called by a loud voice to come to heaven, where the trio of Jesus, Moses, and Elijah would be transfigured in the heavenly realm.

An earthquake destroyed a tenth of the city with 7,000 people dead, and everyone else gave glory to God.

The seventh angel blew his trumpet for the third terror, and there were loud voices shouting in heaven proclaiming the reign of the world by Jesus, the Messiah.

> *The seventh angel sounded his trumpet, and there were loud voices in heaven, which said:*
> *"The kingdom of the world has become*
> *the kingdom of our Lord and of his Messiah,*
> *and he will reign for ever and ever."*—Revelation 11:15

The 24 elders fell to the ground in worship, proclaiming the reign of God and the time of his wrath. They proclaim God's judgment on all who have caused destruction on the earth, and they proclaim God's reward to his servants, the prophets, and his holy people who fear his name, from the least to the greatest. Those who have caused destruction are doomed, and those who revere God will be rewarded.

> *"We give thanks to you, Lord God Almighty,*
> *the One who is and who was,*
> *because you have taken your great power*
> *and have begun to reign.*
> *The nations were angry,*
> *and your wrath has come.*
> *The time has come for judging the dead,*
> *and for rewarding your servants the prophets*
> *and your people who revere your name,*
> *both great and small—*
> *and for destroying those who destroy the earth."* — Revelation 11:17-18

Heaven opened, the Temple of God opened, and the Ark of the Covenant could be seen when the third terror struck. An earthquake and a terrible hailstorm wreak havoc on earth.

John's theme of the nature and identity of God picks up from Chapter 7 in Chapter 11 with descriptors of Jesus and God. Jesus is identified as the Lord's Messiah, who will reign forever, and God is our Lord who reigns over the kingdom of the world, which becomes his kingdom. God's kingdom belongs to both Father God and Son Jesus.

The kingdom of the world has become
the kingdom of our Lord and of his Messiah,
and he will reign for ever and ever." — Revelation 11:15

In the praise by the twenty-four elders in the kingdom of heaven, God is described as mighty, eternal, powerful, judge of the dead, rewarder of his servants like the prophets and his people who revere his name. God is also the destroyer of those who destroy the earth.

We give thanks to you, ***Lord God Almighty,***
the One who is and who was,
because you have taken your ***great power***
and have begun to reign.
The nations were angry,
and your wrath has come.
The time has come for ***judging the dead,***
and for ***rewarding your servants the prophets***
and your people who revere your name,
both great and small—
and for ***destroying those who destroy the earth.***—Revelation 11:17-18

Reflection

1. Imagine prophets whose prophecies matched their prayers so strongly that they could shut the skies so that there would be no rain. Do I know of anyone who has the gift of prophecy and/or prayer that is as powerful as these prophets? What does it take to maintain a prayer life that is this powerful?

2. After the prophets completed their testimony, the beast would kill them, but God would bring them back to life after three and a half days. These prophets, presumably Moses and Elijah, would be resurrected as Jesus was, but through God's power, not their own. Am I prepared to give my testimony of Jesus to the extent that I may be killed, even though God may bring me back to life? Do I have the spiritual courage to testify in the face of death?

3. James 5:17-18, Elijah was described as "praying earnestly." When have I prayed earnestly?

4. What is the shortest prayer of mine that has been answered by God?

5. What is the longest length of time that I have earnestly prayed to God for something or someone?

6. When have I felt the strong presence of the Holy Spirit during my prayer time? What was I praying about? Where and when? How can I design my prayer life to have the time, place, and earnestness to stay in the strong presence of the Holy Spirit?

7. I want to avoid the doom of destruction. What destructive tendencies do I have in my life that need to be changed?

8. I want to be rewarded for revering God. What changes do I need to make to live a life of reverence toward God?

Chapter Twelve

Revelation 12

REVELATION 12: THE WOMAN AND THE DRAGON

John witnesses in heaven a pregnant woman clothed with the sun and the moon beneath her feet,and a crown of 12 stars on her head. She was crying out in labor while a large red dragon with seven heads, seven crowns and ten horns stood ready to devour her baby as soon as it was born. The infant son was to rule all nations with an iron rod and was snatched away from the dragon and caught up to God and his throne. The woman fled to the wilderness where God had prepared a place to care for her for 1,260 days (42 months).

Some people theorize that the woman is Mary, the mother of Jesus, but surely John would have recognized her from his time with Mary and Jesus. Because the woman has a crown of 12 stars, she most likely represented Israel with its 12 tribes. Genesis 37:9 includes one of Joseph's dreams with the sun and the moon and 11 stars bowing down to him.

The baby born of the woman and sent to God and his throne seems most likely to be Jesus.

In 12:7-9, the dragon is identified as the devil or Satan, the one deceiving the whole world. He was thrown out of heaven by Michael and his angels.

> *Then war broke out in heaven. Michael and his angels fought against the dragon, and the dragon and his angels fought back. 8 But he was not strong enough, and they lost their place in heaven. 9 The great dragon was hurled down—that ancient serpent called the devil, or Satan, who leads the whole world astray. He was hurled to the earth, and his angels with him."*
> —Revelation 12:7-9

A loud voice shouts across the heavens that salvation and the Kingdom of our God has come, and the accuser has been thrown down to earth.

> *And they have defeated him by the blood of the Lamb and by their testimony. And they did not love their lives so much that they were afraid to die. Therefore rejoice, you heavens and you who dwell in them! But woe to the earth and the sea, because the devil has gone down to you! He is filled with fury, because he knows that his time is short.*—Revelation 12:11-12

Knowing that he has little time, the devil will create terror on the earth and the sea. When the dragon failed at drowning the woman, he declared war against the rest of her children, defined as all who keep God's commandments and maintain their testimony for Jesus.

As believers covered by the blood of the Lamb and our testimony of Jesus, we have already defeated Satan, although verse 12:11 above implies that we may have to forfeit our lives on earth in the process.

Regarding the theme of the nature and identity of God in Chapter 12, God has the authority to save; he has power, and he is ruler. Son Jesus is God's Messiah, Savior, and Deliverer.

> *Then I heard a loud voice in heaven say: "Now have come the* ***salvation and the power*** *and the* ***kingdom of our God,*** *and the authority of his* <u>*Messiah*</u>*. For the accuser of our brothers and sisters, who accuses them before our God day and night, has been hurled down The seventh angel sounded his trumpet, and there were loud voices in heaven, which said:* —Revelation 12:10

In the very first words spoken to John in this vision of Revelation, the two tenets of purpose were made clear: the word of God and the testimony of his Son, Jesus Christ. Not only were (and are today!) Jesus followers in danger of being killed by the Jews and those opposing the belief that Jesus is the Son of God, but the enemy was out to commit genocide against future generations, i.e. "the rest of her offspring..

> *Then the dragon was enraged at the woman and went off to wage war against the rest of her offspring—**those who keep God's commands and hold fast their testimony about Jesus.***—Revelation 12:17

Reflection

1. Do I accept the idea of a spiritual war being waged by our spiritual enemy of souls? Do I think that I can win this war by keeping God's commandments and maintaining my testimony for Jesus?

2. The devil knows that he has little time to create terror on earth. How much time do I have to remain obedient and to testify for Jesus Christ? Can I afford to waste any time doing anything but following Christ?

3. "And they did not love their lives so much that they were afraid to die." Does this describe me? Do I love my life so much that I am afraid to die? How does Revelation bring consolation to those who fear death?

Chapter Thirteen

Revelation 13

REVELATION 13: THE BEAST OUT OF THE SEA

John sees a beast rising up from the sea who is given his own power and authority by the dragon. One of the seven heads of the beast had been fatally wounded, but the wound was healed. The whole world marveled at this miracle and gave the beast heir allegiance. The world worshiped both the beast and the dragon.

> *People worshiped the dragon because he had given authority to the beast, and they also worshiped the beast and asked, "Who is like the beast? Who can wage war against it?"*—Revelation 13:4

For 42 months, the beast was given authority to do whatever he wanted, including speaking great blasphemies against God and slandering his name, heaven, and those who dwell in heaven. The beast was allowed to conquer God's holy people and to rule over every tribe and people and language and nation.

Verse 13:8 clarifies that all the people who belong to this world worshiped the beast. They are the ones whose names are not written in the Book of Life that belong to the Lamb who was slaughtered before the world was made.

> *All inhabitants of the earth will worship the beast—all whose names have not been written in the Lamb's book of life, the Lamb who was slain from the creation of the world.*—Revelation 13:8

God's timing is not our timing. Since God always was, is, and is to come, the sacrifice of Jesus, the Lamb of God, is noted as happening even before the creation of the world.

In verse 9, a caution to God's holy people is that they "must endure persecution patiently and remain faithful."

John saw another beast coming up out of the earth with all the authority of the first beast. The second beast deceived all the people with miracles and ordered the people to make a great statue of the first beast. Then the statue was brought to life and commanded that anyone refusing to worship it must die. He required everyone to be given a mark on the right hand or on the forehead, which was necessary for them to buy or sell anything. This was the "mark of the beast" that was either the name of the beast or the number representing his name: 666.

The nature and identity of God in Son Jesus is reflected in Revelation 13:8. Jesus, as the Lamb of God, holds a book of people's names, those who are granted eternal life. Jesus is the one who was slain, that is, crucified on the cross, from the creation of the world. His role as the redeeming, sacrificial lamb was established from the beginning of creation through the authority of God the Creator.

> *All inhabitants of the earth will worship the beast—all whose names have not been written in the Lamb's book of life, the Lamb who was slain from the creation of the world.*—Revelation 12:10

In the very first words spoken to John in this vision of Revelation, the two tenets of purpose were made clear: the word of God and the testimony of his Son, Jesus Christ. Not only were (and are today!) Jesus followers in danger of being killed by the Jews and those opposing the belief that Jesus is the Son of God, but the enemy was out to commit genocide against future generations, i.e. "the rest of her offspring..

> *Then the dragon was enraged at the woman and went off to wage war against the rest of her offspring—**those who keep God's commands and hold fast their testimony about Jesus.***—Revelation 12:17

Reflection

1. Have I ever spoken blasphemy of God's name, heaven, or those in heaven? Have I used God's name in disrespectful terms? Have I failed to give God the glory that is due him?

2. Have I repented for my words of disrespect or profanity that were based in the name of God?

3. There is a clear delineation of people divided into "people who belonged to this world" and "people whose names are in the Book of Life." Can I definitively place my name in one of these two groups? If I "belong to this world" in areas of finances, politics, arts and entertainment, careers, or social groups, what do I need to do to change? If I want to be confident that my name will be in the Book of Life, by what standards would I measure my thoughts, words, actions?

4. What clear signs in the world reveal that Satan is at work in gathering people to receive his mark of the beast?

5. With whose name do I claim all authority over Satan and the evil of this world? How often do I praise the name of God and pray "in the name of Jesus"?

CHAPTER FOURTEEN

Revelation 14

REVELATION 14: THE LAMB AND THE 144,000

John saw the Lamb appear on Mount Zion with 144,000 who are marked, but his redeemed are marked with the name of the Lamb and his Father's name on their foreheads. A thunderous orchestra of harps is heard with a great choir of the 144,000 redeemed singing a new song in front of the throne of God. This song is one that only they could learn, these redeemed who have told no lies and are without blame.

Three angels appear in succession. One carried the eternal Good News to proclaim to people who belong to the world–to every nation, tribe, language, and people. The angel shouted for all to give glory to God because the time had come for him to sit as judge.

The second angel followed, shouting, "Babylon is fallen", and the third angel followed, shouting eternal torture for anyone worshiping the beast, his statue, or wearing his mark on the forehead or hand.

From the three angels, we get the eternal Good News, the bad news of Babylon's fall, and the eternal bad news of eternal torment with no relief for those accepting the mark of the beast.

Verse 12 advises God's holy people that they must endure persecution patiently, that they must obey his commands, and that they must maintain their faith in Jesus. Those who die in the Lord will find rest for their good deeds.

In verse 14, John saw the Son of Man with a gold crown and sharp sickle coming on a white cloud. A fourth angel came from the Temple shouting for him to swing his sickle for the harvest. The Son of Man, the title for Jesus himself, proceeded to swing his sickle over the whole earth harvesting it.

A fifth angel came from the Temple with a sharp sickle and gathered the clusters of grapes from the vines of the earth. He loaded the grapes into the great winepress of God's wrath, and blood flowed from the winepress for great lengths and heights.

Jesus himself prophesied the harvest of souls when he taught through parables to his disciples. The harvest in the parable names angels as harvesters, and Revelation 14:19 describes the angel harvesting the earth of evil. As John saw and listened to this part of the Revelation, certainly he would have remembered Jesus' parables about the harvest.

> *"He answered, "The one who sowed the good seed is the Son of Man. The field is the world, and the good seed stands for the people of the kingdom. The weeds are the people of the evil one, and the enemy who sows them is the devil. The harvest is the end of the age, and the harvesters are angels.*
>
> *"As the weeds are pulled up and burned in the fire, so it will be at the end of the age. The Son of Man will send out his angels, and they will weed out of his kingdom everything that causes sin and all who do evil.*
>
> *They will throw them into the blazing furnace, where there will be weeping and gnashing of teeth. 43 Then the righteous will shine like the sun in the kingdom of their Father. Whoever has ears, let them hear"* —Matthew 13:37-43

Then the angels and elders and four living beings worship God in song:

> *"Amen! Blessing and glory and wisdom,*
> *Thanksgiving and honor and power and might,*
> *Be to our God forever and ever.*
> *Amen."*—Revelation 7:12

Regarding the nature and identity of God in Revelation, Jesus is identified in this chapter as the Lamb of God, standing on Mount Zion.

> *Then I looked, and there before me was the Lamb, standing on Mount Zion, and with him 144,000 who had his name and his Father's name written on their foreheads.*—Revelation 14:1

Jesus' position on Mount Zion in this prophecy is significant because of other biblical occurrences on Mount Zion:

- The first temple
- Abraham's place of sacrifice of his son, Isaac
- Jacob's dream
- Solomon's temple
- City of David (Ark of the Covenant)
- City of Jerusalem
- Jewish nation

An angel in a loud voice declares that God, the Creator, is to be revered, feared. He is to receive glory. He is judge over creation. He made the heavens, the earth, the seas, and the springs of water.

> *He said in a loud voice, "**Fear God and give him glory,** because the hour of **his judgment** has come. **Worship him who made the heavens, the earth, the sea and the springs of water.**"*—Revelation 14:7

In Revelation 14:14, Jesus is the Son of Man, the same nomenclature given to both Daniel and Jesus in Daniel's dream, a connection of them both being human and descendants of Adam, as well as prophets concerning end times. Jesus has authority, as indicated by the crown of gold, and he has the power to judge or harvest, as indicated by his sharp sickle.

> *"In my vision at night I looked, and there before me was one like a son of man, coming with the clouds of heaven. He approached the Ancient of Days and was led into his presence. 14 He was given authority, glory and sovereign power; all nations and peoples of every language worshiped him. His dominion is an everlasting dominion that will not pass away, and his kingdom is one that will never be destroyed."*—Daniel 7:13-14

> *As he came near the place where I was standing, I was terrified and fell prostrate. "Son of man," he said to me, "understand that the vision concerns the time of the end."*—Daniel 8:-17

> *I looked, and there before me was a white cloud, and seated on the cloud was one like a son of man with a crown of gold on his head and a sharp sickle in his hand."*—Revelation14:14

have the total protection and provision of God. In heaven, there is no hunger, thirst, discomfort of the elements, or sadness. As the Lamb of God, Jesus is seated at the center of the throne and acts as their shepherd.

Reflection

1. How do I endure persecution patiently?

2. What accountability have I built into my life that helps me to obey all of God's commands?

3. How do I maintain my faith in Jesus? Do I stay grounded in the Word? Do I pray earnestly? Do I testify to others about my faith? Do I remember and/or record all the blessings and miracles in my life to build my faith in Jesus? Do I remember my life before believing in Jesus and acknowledge my life now as a believer in Jesus?

4. When it comes time for the harvest, will I be entangled in the weeds to be pulled, or will I be flourishing in a field of strong, healthy Christians?

5. The angels will come to "weed out every sin" and "all who do evil". What sin do I need to weed out right now, should the harvest time be today?

CHAPTER FIFTEEN

Revelation 15

REVELATION 15: THE SONG OF MOSES AND THE SONG OF THE LAMB

John saw in heaven seven angels holding the seven last plagues that would complete God's wrath upon the earth. Those who were victorious over the beast and his statue were holding harps that God had given them.

> *And I saw what looked like a sea of glass glowing with fire and, standing beside the sea, those who had been victorious over the beast and its image and over the number of its name. They held harps given them by God.*
> —Revelation 15:2

Revelation 15:3 records that the people were singing the song of Moses and the song of the Lamb. This song of Moses was first sung in victory over the Egyptians after crossing the Red Sea, as recorded in Exodus 15.

Psalm 90 is a song written and delivered by Moses acknowledging God's favor as well as God's wrath that is to come.

In Deuteronomy 32, near his death, Moses created a song for people of Israel with a promise of vengeance and atonement by God. Here is part of that song.

> *See now that I myself am he!*
> *There is no god besides me.*
> *I put to death and I bring to life,*
> *I have wounded and I will heal,*
> *and no one can deliver out of my hand.*
>
> *I lift my hand to heaven and solemnly swear:*
> *As surely as I live forever,*
>
> *when I sharpen my flashing sword*
> *and my hand grasps it in judgment,*
> *I will take vengeance on my adversaries*
> *and repay those who hate me.*
>
> *I will make my arrows drunk with blood,*
> *while my sword devours flesh:*
> *the blood of the slain and the captives,*
> *the heads of the enemy leaders."*
>
> *Rejoice, you nations, with his people,*
> *for he will avenge the blood of his servants;*

he will take vengeance on his enemies
and make atonement for his land and people.
—Deuteronomy 32:39-43

John saw God's Tabernacle was thrown wide open, and there were seven angels with the seven plagues. No one could enter the Temple until the seven angels had completed pouring out the seven plagues, described in the next chapter.

In this chapter concerning God's nature and identity, seven angels describe God described as great, marvelous, just, true, king of the nations, holy, and righteous. God must have all these qualities of character in order to justly command fear of his people and to righteously judge people according to their actions. God also is worthy of the praise of his angels.

Seven angels with the seven last plagues play the harps and sing:
"Great and marvelous are your deeds,
Lord God Almighty.
***Just and true** are your ways,*
King of the nations.
Who will not fear you, Lord,
and bring glory to your name?
*For **you alone are holy.***
All nations will come
and worship before you,
*for your **righteous acts** have been revealed.".*—Revelation 15:3-4

Reflection

1. If I had a song of victory like Moses, what would my lyrics be? (Try writing your own song of victory and praise for what God has done for you.)

2. What does it feel like to be a part of a plague during my lifetime? How do I feel, knowing that I have endured and survived a plague? How much thanksgiving have I given to God for saving my life, my soul, my family?

Chapter Sixteen

Revelation 16

REVELATION 16: THE SEVEN PLAGUES

1. Malignant sores broke out on everyone with the mark of the beast who worshiped his statue.

2. Everything in the sea died.

3. Rivers and springs became blood.

4. The sun scorched everyone with its fire. Everyone was burnt and cursed God, refusing to repent and turn to God.

   The angel of the third plague declares that God sent these judgments because they shed the blood of his holy people and his prophets. "You have given them blood to drink. It is their just reward."—Revelation 15:2

5. The beast's kingdom was plunged into darkness, and his subjects cursed God and did not repent of their evil deeds.

6. The great Euphrates River dried up so that the kings from the east could march their armies toward the west without hindrance. The demonic spirits gathered all the rulers and their armies in a place called "Armageddon."

7. A great earthquake struck, the worst since people were placed on the earth. Babylon split into three sections; many nations' cities fell into heaps of rubble; islands disappeared; and all the mountains were leveled.

Because of the hailstorm with hailstones weighing 75 pounds, people cursed God.

With the seventh and final plague, a mighty shout from the throne in the Temple said, "It is finished!" The number seven is the number of completion. God had completed all the plagues that were to fall on the earth.

Regarding the nature and identity of God, consistent descriptors of God continue: just, holy, eternal, Lord, all mighty, and true. Only God, who in his nature is pure and righteous, can judge righteously those who have shed the blood of his holy people and prophets.

Then I heard the angel in charge of the waters say:
*"You are **just** in these judgments, O **Holy** One,*
you who are and who were;
or they have shed the blood of your holy people and your prophets,
and you have given them blood to drink as they deserve."

And I heard the altar respond:
*"Yes, **Lord God Almighty,***
***true** and **just** are your judgments."*—Revelation 16:5-7

It is also God's nature to remember. Not only does God remember us and our prayers through eternity, God also remembers those who do evil and repays them with the fury of his wrath.

Psalm 90 is a song written and delivered by Moses acknowledging God's favor as well as God's wrath that is to come.

In Deuteronomy 32, near his death, Moses created a song for people of Israel with a promise of vengeance and atonement by God. Here is part of that song.

God remembered** Babylon the Great and **gave her the cup filled with the wine of the fury of his wrath. —Revelation 16:9

Reflection

1. **Our world has been through plagues, droughts, war, earthquakes, wildfires, hailstorms, and religious persecutions. How tempting would it be to curse God as the cause of our problems? How comforting is it to know that, regardless of the death and destruction on earth, I can look forward to eternal life in heaven with God? Describe your feelings about the comfort you have in God's promise of eternal life.**

2. **At some point in my life, I will be able to say that my life is finished. How will I look back on my life? What regrets will I have? What victories will I have? Will I be prepared to see Jesus in peace and contentment?**

Chapter Seventeen

Revelation 17

REVELATION 17: THE GREAT PROSTITUTE

One of the seven angels takes John to the wilderness to see the judgment that is going to come upon the great prostitute, identified as "Babylon the Great, Mother of All Prostitutes and Obscenities in the World." She was seated on a scarlet beast that had seven heads and ten horns, and blasphemies against God written all over it. She was drunk with the blood of God's holy people who were witnesses for Jesus. The seven heads represent the seven hills and the seven kings where the woman rules. Five kings have fallen, the sixth reigns now, and the seventh is yet to come for a brief reign. The scarlet beast is the eighth king. The ten horns of the beast are the ten kings who have not yet risen to power. They will agree to give the beast their power and authority.

> *I saw that the woman was drunk with the blood of God's holy people, the blood of those who bore* ***testimony to Jesus.****"*—Revelation 17:6

> *They will wage war against the Lamb, but the Lamb will triumph over them because he is Lord of lords and King of kings—and with him will be his called, chosen and faithful followers.*—Revelation 17:14

The angel tells John that the scarlet beast and his ten horns all hate the prostitute. He says they will strip her naked, eat her flesh, and burn her remains with fire. The angel said that all this is according to God's plan, even when evil versus evil.

> *For God has put it into their hearts to accomplish his purpose by agreeing to hand over to the beast their royal authority, until God's words are fulfilled. 18 The woman you saw is the great city that rules over the kings of the earth.*—Revelation 17:18

Reflection

1. What is happening in the world around me that appears to be the working of reigning kings, fallen kings, misplaced power and authority?

2. The Lamb will triumph with his called, chosen, faithful followers. Do I feel called by Jesus? Do I feel chosen by God? Am I a faithful follower? Do I feel that I am a part of this victory over evil?

Chapter Eighteen

Revelation 18

REVELATION 18: THE FALL OF BABYLON

Because of the hailstorm with hailstones weighing 75 pounds, people cursed Another angel gave a mighty shout about the fall of Babylon. Then John heard another voice calling from heaven to tell God's people to stay away from Babylon. The voice announced God's judgment with the plagues that would overtake Babylon in a single day – death and mourning and famine – followed by being completely consumed by fire.

No consumers were left to buy the goods from the merchants of the world. Babylon had bought great quantities of gems, expensive things, livestock, and bodies, including human slaves. The merchants mourned their losses. Babylon could represent governing bodies, businesses, religions, or any profitable organized groups growing rich through acts of adultery, immorality, idolatry, and desires for extravagant luxuries.

Following the mourning of the merchants came the rejoicing of the people of God, apostles, and prophets that God's judgment had come.

> *Rejoice over her, you heavens!*
> *Rejoice, you people of God!*
> *Rejoice, apostles and prophets!*
> *For God has judged her*
> *with the judgment she imposed on you."*—Revelation 18:20

A mighty angel picked up a boulder and threw it into the ocean, and shouted:

> *"With such violence*
> *the great city of Babylon will be thrown down,*
> *never to be found again.*
>
> *Your merchants were the world's important people.*
> *By your magic spell all the nations were led astray.*
>
> *In her was found the blood of prophets and of God's holy people,*
> *of all who have been slaughtered on the earth." God remembered Babylon the Great and gave her the cup filled with the wine of the fury of his wrath.*—Revelation 18:21, 23b-24

Continuing the theme of God's nature and identity, God is Judge. God judges the city of Babylon as its kings judged the people of God. The kings of the earth and the merchants of the earth cry woes as the city of Babylon falls under the judgment of God:

> *Therefore in one day her plagues will overtake her:*
> *death, mourning and famine.*
> *She will be consumed by fire,*
> *for* ***mighty is the Lord God who judges her.***—Revelation 18:8

> *""Rejoice over her, you heavens!*
> *Rejoice, you people of God!*
> *Rejoice, apostles and prophets!*
> *For* ***God has judged her***
> ***with the judgment she imposed on you."***—Revelation 18:8

Reflection

1. God's people were warned to stay away from Babylon because it was going to undergo plagues and then it was going to be consumed by fire. In my life, God has given me warnings to stay away from evil people, places, and things. How successful have I been at keeping my life free from being negatively impacted by the evil in the world? How can I insulate my soul from the world's influences?

2. By my spending habits, do I support businesses who promote acts of adultery, immorality, idolatry, and desires for extravagant luxuries? Do I support businesses who fund abortion clinics, satanic articles, magic, excessive materialism? If so, what changes do I need to make?

3. Who represents Babylon in today's world?

Chapter Nineteen

Revelation 19

REVELATION 19: THREE-FOLD SONGS OF VICTORY IN HEAVEN

John heard the vast crowd in heaven shouting praises to God for his vengeance that began as a roar of a great multitude and swelled to a sound like rushing water and loud peals of thunder. Imagine standing outside of the cathedral where British royalty have just gotten married, and the bells are ringing with a crowd of thousands shouting their allegiance and joy to the royal couple. This sound would be many decibels lower than the sound that John heard by the vast crowd in heaven praising God. Can we really imagine just how loud and victorious this sound of praise would be?

> *"After this I heard what sounded like the roar of a great multitude in heaven shouting:*
> *"Hallelujah!*
> *Salvation and glory and power belong to our God,*
>
> *for true and just are his judgments.*
> *He has condemned the great prostitute*
> *who corrupted the earth by her adulteries.*
> *He has avenged on her the blood of his servants."*
>
> *And again they shouted:*
> *"Hallelujah!*
> *The smoke from her goes up for ever and ever."*
>
> *The twenty-four elders and the four living creatures fell down and worshiped God, who was seated on the throne. And they cried:*
> *"Amen, Hallelujah!"*
>
> *Then a voice came from the throne, saying:*
> *"Praise our God,*
> *all you his servants,*
> *you who fear him,*
> *both great and small!"*
>
> *Then I heard what sounded like a great multitude, like the roar of rushing waters and like loud peals of thunder, shouting:*
> *"Hallelujah!*
> *For our Lord God Almighty reigns.*
>
> *Let us rejoice and be glad*
> *and give him glory!*

> *For the wedding of the Lamb has come,*
> *and his bride has made herself ready.*
>
> *Fine linen, bright and clean,*
> *was given her to wear."*—Revelation 19:1-8

In verse 9, the angel tells John to write the true words from God: "Blessed are those who are invited to the wedding feast of the Lamb."

John would have understood the great significance of the wedding feast of the Lamb from Jesus' parables told to his disciples and then recorded in Matthew 22:1-14 and Luke 14:15-24.

John is so overwhelmed that he falls down to worship the angel, but the angel reminds him to worship only God. And then the angel states the reason for this prophecy that John has received:

> *"At this I fell at his feet to worship him. But he said to me, "Don't do that! I am a fellow servant with you and with your brothers and sisters who hold to* ***the testimony of Jesus****. Worship God! For it is the Spirit of prophecy who bears* ***testimony to Jesus****."*—Revelation 19:10

These two sentences summarize all that we are to do: to worship God and hold to the testimony of Jesus. We are to be witnesses for Jesus, the Son of God.

In verse 11, John saw heaven opened and a white horse with a rider named Faithful and True. His robe had been dipped in blood and his title was the Word of God; on his robe at his thigh was the title, King of all kings and Lord of all lords. Armies in heaven followed him. He was to release the wrath of God like blood flowing from a winepress.

An angel called for a gathering for the great banquet God prepared, a banquet of the flesh of kings and generals, strong warriors, and all humanity, both free and slave, great and small.

> *And I saw an angel standing in the sun, who cried in a loud voice to all the birds flying in midair, "Come, gather together for the great supper of God, 18 so that you may eat the flesh of kings, generals, and the mighty, of horses and their riders, and the flesh of all people, free and slave, great and small."*—Revelation 19:7-8

Then the rider on the white horse defeats the beast and the kings of the world, along with the false prophet who did mighty miracles. Their entire army was killed by the sharp sword that came from the mouth of the rider on the white horse. This is Jesus, as described in Revelation 1:16 and 2:12.

Since the title of the rider is the Word of God and the entire army is killed by the sharp sword that came from his mouth, these verses affirm the power of the Word of God to convict, judge, and defeat those who fall to the lies and falsehood of false prophets.

Regarding the nature and identity of God in Revelation, in Chapter 19, salvation, glory, and power are God's. At Babylon's fall, the multitudes of heaven rejoice and give praise to God. He is true and just. He condemns evil and he avenges his servants' blood sacrifice. God reigns almighty.

> *"Hallelujah!*
> ***Salvation and glory and power belong to our God,***
>
> *for **true and just** are his judgments.*
> *He has **condemned** the great prostitute*
> *who corrupted the earth by her adulteries.*
> *He has **avenged** on her the blood of his servants."*—Revelation 19:1-2

> *"Hallelujah!*
> *For our **Lord God Almighty reigns.**"*—Revelation 19:6 (part)

Following this description of God, the Avenger, comes a majestic description of Jesus, the Avenger: God the Father and Jesus the Son acting as One God. Jesus comes from heaven with the name "Faithful and True" and rides a white horse. He comes to judge and to wage war on the wicked. With eyes ablaze and head crowned, he wears a robe dipped in blood. From his mouth is a sharp sword, and he embodies every truth of Scripture, as his name is "the Word of God". The image of Jesus treading a winepress indicates the total fury of the wrath of God, just as a winepress squeezes out the last bit of juice from every grape. Both on his robe and on his thigh is written the magnificent title for Jesus: King of Kings and Lord of Lords. John's writing leaves no doubt that Jesus reigns.

> *"I saw heaven standing open and there before me was a white horse, whose rider is called Faithful and True. With justice he judges and wages war.*

His eyes are like blazing fire, and on his head are many crowns. He has a name written on him that no one knows but he himself. He is dressed in a robe dipped in blood, and his name is the Word of God. The armies of heaven were following him, riding on white horses and dressed in fine linen, white and clean. Coming out of his mouth is a sharp sword with which to strike down the nations. "He will rule them with an iron scepter." He treads the winepress of the fury of the wrath of God Almighty. On his robe and on his thigh he has this name written:

KING OF KINGS AND LORD OF LORDS.—Revelation 19:11-16

Reflection

1. As Christ prepares for the wedding feast, how prepared is the church today to be the bride of Christ? Does Jesus see his church as pure, holy, and worthy to be his bride? What changes need to be made in the church before becoming the worthy Bride of Christ? What is Christ expecting of his bride?

2. In this chapter are references to a wedding feast for the bride of Christ, his church; and a banquet of the flesh when the scavenger birds will consume the flesh of the kings and all who fought against the King of Kings and the Armies of Heaven. Which "Lord's Supper" do I plan to attend? How do I know which invitation I will receive

Chapter Twenty

Revelation 20

REVELATION 20: THE THOUSAND YEARS

In this vision, John saw those who were martyred for their faith in Jesus and for sharing the word of God. Since John lived at the same time as Jesus' life and death on the cross, is it possible that he would recognize the faces of the souls who had been beheaded? Or were the souls transfigured in the glory of heaven, and John saw the souls "in the Spirit" and knew who they were? When we read verses like 20:4, we have an historic perspective that makes the vision so surreal, but John was there! He was "living the dream" or "living the nightmare" of being a Jesus follower under persecution. John's hope and faith is increased by this vision of seeing the martyrs seated on God's throne, even with authority to judge! Knowing the reward of heaven was waiting for him, and that justice was waiting for his enemies, John's perseverance and courage must have helped him to sustain his exile and future mission for the early church..

> *I saw thrones on which were seated those who had been given authority to judge. And I saw the souls of those who had been beheaded because of their* ***testimony about Jesus and because of the word of God.*** *They had not worshiped the beast or its image and had not received its mark on their foreheads or their hands. They came to life and reigned with Christ a thousand years. 5 (The rest of the dead did not come to life until the thousand years were ended.) This is the first resurrection."* —Revelation 16:5-7

With the key to the bottomless pit and a heavy chain, an angel came down from heaven and seized the dragon, identified here as the old serpent, the devil, Satan. After 1,000 years, he was to be released again for "a little while."

> *He seized the dragon, that ancient serpent, who is the devil, or* ***Satan,*** *and bound him for a thousand years.*—Revelation 20:6

Then John saw "the first resurrection" of the souls who had been beheaded for their testimony about Jesus and for proclaiming the word of God. They reigned with Christ for 1,000 years. The rest of the dead came back to life after the 1,000 year reign. Verse 6 states:

> *Blessed and holy are those who share in the first resurrection. The second death has no power over them, but they will be priests of God and of Christ*

> *and will reign with him for a thousand years.*—Revelation 20:2

Following the 1,000 year reign, Satan was let out of prison, who gathered his armies for battle, but a fire from heaven came down and consumed them. The devil was thrown into a fiery lake, joining the beast and the false prophet, and they will be tormented day and night forever and ever.

> *When the thousand years are over,* ***Satan*** *will be released from his prison and will go out to deceive the nations in the four corners of the earth—Gog and Magog—and to gather them for battle. In number they are like the sand on the seashore. They marched across the breadth of the earth and surrounded the camp of God's people, the city he loves. But fire came down from heaven and devoured them. And the* ***devil,*** *who deceived them, was thrown into the lake of burning sulfur, where the beast and the false prophet had been thrown. They will be tormented day and night for ever and ever.*—Revelation 20:7-10

John saw the final judgment of souls, judged according to their deeds. The books were opened, including the Book of Life. The doomed were thrown into the fiery lake, and the redeemed were to join the new heaven and new earth, as described in the next chapter.

Reflection

1. **Am I living in a world that seems as though souls are reigning with Christ, or am I living in a world that seems to be ruled by Satan? What is the evidence for either argument?**

2. **If I am to be judged according to my deeds in the final judgment of souls, what deeds will be listed? Are there any that I want to add? Are there any for which I need to repent?**

Chapter Twenty-One

Revelation 21

REVELATION 21: THE NEW JERUSALEM

The first seven verses of this chapter describe God's creation of a new heaven and earth as a total re-do, a total re-creation of what he had made in Genesis. One would think that God would only need to recreate the earth with all his purging of sin by death and destruction, but John saw a new heaven as well. Since God's plan is to dwell among his people, heaven and earth seem to be merged as one. There is no reason to have heaven and earth separated. In this Holy City, called the new Jerusalem, the setting seems like a renewed Garden of Eden, where God walked with Adam and Eve before their sin. Since the devil, the beast, the false prophets and their followers remain in the fiery lake of burning sulfur, there is no contamination as there was when Satan was cast out of the first heaven. This new setting for God and his people is totally pure and free from sin.

Along with a brand new place to dwell together, there is an absence of death, mourning, crying, and pain in the hearts and souls of God's people. The new order of God's creation dispels any form of negative emotions or experiences for eternity. These seven verses are the hope on which we can cling through any diversity that we experience in the "old earth" where we presently dwell. In verse 7, God's covenant is restated as he has told us through all of history that he will be our God and we will be his people.

> *"Then I saw "a new heaven and a new earth," for the first heaven and the first earth had passed away, and there was no longer any sea. I saw the Holy City, the new Jerusalem, coming down out of heaven from God, prepared as a bride beautifully dressed for her husband. And I heard a loud voice from the throne saying, "Look! God's dwelling place is now among the people, and he will dwell with them. They will be his people, and God himself will be with them and be their God. 'He will wipe every tear from their eyes. There will be no more death or mourning or crying or pain, for the old order of things has passed away."*
>
> *He who was seated on the throne said, "I am making everything new!" Then he said, "Write this down, for these words are trustworthy and true."*
>
> *He said to me: "It is done. I am the Alpha and the Omega, the Beginning and the End. To the thirsty I will give water without cost from the spring of the water of life. 7 Those who are victorious will inherit all this, and* <u>*I will*</u>

be their God and they will be my children.—Revelation 21:1-6

Through the Bible, we read that God has made a covenant between him and his people. From Adam to Noah to Abraham, Moses, Joshua, David, Solomon, Jeremiah, and Jesus' disciples, God has promised that he will be our God, and we will be his people.

In Genesis 2:15-17, God instructed Adam and Eve. In Genesis 3:8, God first walked in the Garden of Eden where they walked.

In Genesis 6:18, God told Noah that he would establish a covenant with him and commissioned the ark.

In Genesis 17:1-2, God told Abraham to walk before him faithfully, and Abraham would be the father of generations to come.

In Exodus 3, God appeared to Moses in a fiery bush, in the cloud, and on the mountain.

In Joshua 1:9, God promised to be with Joshua wherever he went.

In 2 Samuel 7:8-16, God promises to be David's father and David to be his son.

In 1 Chronicles 28:9, David passed down God's covenant promises to David's son, Solomon. God would be with him if he would seek God with all his heart. Fulfilling this promise, in 2 Chronicles 7, God's presence filled the temple of Solomon.

In Jeremiah 7:22-29, God reminds Jeremiah of God's covenant with his people if they would obey.

In Matthew 28, God's Son, Jesus, walked with his disciples to teach them the way to eternal life, and he said to them, "And surely I am with you always, to the very end of the age."

In Paul's letter to the Hebrews, Paul describes God's new covenant through Jesus Christ.

> *"But in fact the ministry Jesus has received is as superior to theirs as the covenant of which he is mediator is superior to the old one, since the new covenant is established on better promises. For if there had been nothing*

wrong with that first covenant, no place would have been sought for another. But God found fault with the people and said:

"The days are coming, declares the Lord,
when I will make a new covenant
with the people of Israel
and with the people of Judah.

It will not be like the covenant
I made with their ancestors
when I took them by the hand
to lead them out of Egypt,
because they did not remain faithful to my covenant,
and I turned away from them,
declares the Lord.

This is the covenant I will establish with the people of Israel
after that time, declares the Lord.
I will put my laws in their minds
and write them on their hearts.
I will be their God,
and they will be my people.

No longer will they teach their neighbor,
or say to one another, 'Know the Lord,'
because they will all know me,
from the least of them to the greatest.

For I will forgive their wickedness
and will remember their sins no more."

By calling this covenant "new," he has made the first one obsolete; and what is obsolete and outdated will soon disappear."—Hebrews 8:6-13

Finally, in the book of Revelation, God's covenant will be fulfilled as Jesus returns for his church, his bride, and God will come and dwell among his people in the new Jerusalem.

Revelation 21 describes the holy city, Jerusalem, descending out of heaven. Exact measurements are given, just as exact measurements were given for Solomon to build God's temple. The walls of the new Jerusalem have foundation stones inlaid with twelve precious stones, presumably meaning the twelve tribes of Israel and/or the twelve disciples of Jesus. This new city needs no temple, for God is the temple as he dwells with his people. The city needs no light, for God illuminates the city, and the Lamb is its light. The gates remain open because there is no night and no need to be protected from any harm nor any sinful people. There are none. The citizens of the new Jerusalem are those whose names are written in the Lamb's Book of Life. The book has closed, and the gates have been opened forever.

Regarding the nature and identity of God, in this chapter we see the most personal character of God, one who desires to dwell with his people and who will comfort those who have suffered.

> *And I heard a loud voice from the throne saying, "Look! God's dwelling place is now among the people, and* ***he will dwell with them.*** *They will be his people, and* ***God himself will be with them and be their God.*** *'He will wipe every tear from their eyes."*—Revelation 21:3

God is pictured on the throne as a Creator, ReCreator, King, and Father. God says that he makes everything new. He himself says that his words are trustworthy and true. He describes himself as the Alpha and Omega, the Beginning and the End. He gives life, and he will be God and Father to the victorious who inherit eternity because they are his children.

> ***He who was seated on the throne*** *said, "I am* ***making everything new!"*** *Then he said, "Write this down, for these* ***words are trustworthy and true."***
>
> *He said to me: "It is done. I am the* ***Alpha and the Omega, the Beginning and the End.*** *To the thirsty* ***I will give water without cost from the spring of the water of life.*** *Those who are* ***victorious*** *will inherit all this, and* ***I will be their God and they will be my children."***—Revelation 21:5-7

With God is the title Lord and Almighty. Jesus is the Lamb of God. Both are the temple of the new Jerusalem with no need for an earthly structure for a temple. God provides light by his glory, and Jesus provides the lamp for the light.

> *I did not see a temple in the city, because the* ***Lord God Almighty*** *and* ***the Lamb are its temple.*** *The city does not need the sun or the moon to shine on it, for the* ***glory of God gives it light,*** *and the Lamb is its lamp.*
> —Revelation 21:22-23

Reflection

1. What will it be like to have God as the temple with no need for a physical structure? How does this align with our bodies being God's temple?

2. God's plan has always been to dwell with his people. What opportunities do I have to invite God to dwell among us? Do I feel God's spirit within me, at work around me, protecting me, guiding me?

3. Imagine an absence of death, mourning, crying, and pain forever. How does that give me hope in the presence of pain and suffering?

4. As God's plan to "make everything new," how can I start this process now to make myself a "new" and "improved" follower of Jesus?

5. If the Lamb is the light, how can I share the light of Jesus with others so that they can be a part of the new Jerusalem?

Chapter Twenty-Two

Revelation 22

REVELATION 22: COME, LORD JESUS!

The angel showed John a river with the water of life flowing from the throne of God and of the Lamb down the center of the main street. (It seems every city has a main street, even New Jerusalem!) On each side grew a tree of life with twelve crops of fruit, and the leaves were used for medicine to heal. Not only had God created a new heaven and a new earth, for his people he ensured a process for healing the nations.

There would be no more curse upon anything, only blessings by being in the presence of the Lord God forever. The angel assured John that everything that he had seen and heard was trustworthy and true.

> *"The angel said to me, "These words are trustworthy and true. The Lord, the God who inspires the prophets, sent his angel to show his servants the things that must soon take place."*
>
> *"Look, I am coming **soon**! Blessed is the one who keeps the words of the prophecy written in this scroll.*—Revelation 22:6-7

Through the book of Revelation, Jesus said that he is coming soon. The word "soon" is a relative term with no specific time passage, other than it being the opposite of "later." Whatever God's or Jesus' idea of "soon" is, no one knows when the end time will come to pass.

The word "soon" is mentioned in the following chapters of the book of Revelation:

> *"The revelation from Jesus Christ, which God gave him to show his servants what must **soon** take place. He made it known by sending his angel to his servant John.*—Revelation 1:1
>
> *Repent therefore! Otherwise, I will **soon** come to you and will fight against them with the sword of my mouth.*—Revelation 2:16
>
> *I am coming **soon**. Hold on to what you have, so that no one will take your crown.*—Revelation 3:11
>
> *The second woe has passed; the third woe is coming soon.*—Revelation 3:14
>
> *The angel said to me, "These words are trustworthy and true. The Lord, the*

> *God who inspires the prophets, sent his angel to show his servants the things that must **soon** take place."*—Revelation 22:6
>
> *"Look, I am coming **soon**! Blessed is the one who keeps the words of the prophecy written in this scroll."*—Revelation 22:7
>
> *"Look, I am coming **soon**! My reward is with me, and I will give to each person according to what they have done.*—Revelation 22:12
>
> *He who testifies to these things says, "Yes, I am coming **soon**-." Amen. Come, Lord Jesus.*—Revelation 22:20

Even though we do not know when the time is coming for Jesus to return or for God to judge the earth with his wrath, the use of the word "soon" emphasizes the urgency for the hearers and readers of this prophecy to make haste. Make haste to repent. Make haste to share the Word of God with others. Make haste to follow all of God's instructions. Make haste in preparing for our last days, either our individual last days on earth or everyone's last days on earth with his second coming.

Whenever I say goodbye to my toddler grandbabies, I give them a hug and a kiss and say, "I'll see you soon!" Because their concept of days, weeks, and months is not yet fully developed, they are happy with the idea that sometime in the near future, we will see each other again. Or they will ask me when they can come to my house again, and I will say, "Soon!" because the intent is there, but the details have not yet been worked out with my schedule and their parents' schedule. When Jesus says that he is coming soon, could it be that our concept of time in the construct of eternity is not yet fully developed? Or might Jesus be waiting for the details of salvation to be worked out with all those who still have the opportunity to make the decision to follow him.

> 2 Peter 3:9 states, *"The Lord is not slow about His promise, as some count slowness, but is patient toward you, not wishing for any to perish but for all to come to repentance."*

Jesus says in verse 7, "Look, I am coming soon! Blessed is the one who keeps the words of the prophecy written in this scroll." John testifies that he is the one who heard and saw all these things. Once again, when John wanted to fall at the feet of the angel who delivered this prophecy, the angel reminded him, "No, don't worship me. I am a servant of God, just like you and your brothers the prophets, as well as all who obey what is written in this book. Worship only God!"

We join with John and the prophets as the hearers of this prophecy who are to obey God's Word.

> *Then he told me, "Do not seal up the words of the prophecy of this scroll, because the time is near. 11 Let the one who does wrong continue to do wrong; let the vile person continue to be vile; let the one who does right continue to do right; and let the holy person continue to be holy."*
> —Revelation 22:10-11

Again, the time frame is soon or "near" so that we stand firm in a life of righteousness. Verse 11 reminds us that we will always have people doing wrong. Evil will exist in this world until New Jerusalem arrives, but that should not deter us from our paths of righteous living.

Jesus again identifies himself as the Alpha and the Omega, the First and the Last, the Beginning and the End. Jesus is eternal in nature, and his present nature, his transfigured form, is the Jesus we will see face-to-face. He is still with us.

Verse 14 repeats the blessing that comes to those who wash their robes and will be permitted entrance into the gates of the city. On the other hand, outside the city will remain the sorcerers, the sexually immoral, the murderers, and idol worshippers, and all who "love to live a lie." That expression of loving to live a lie perfectly describes a person who lives in sin but deceives himself/herself that there is no need for repentance.

Verse 16 is another identifier of Jesus when he calls himself both the source of David and the heir to his throne. He is the bright morning star. From his roots in the line of David to the heights of the heavens, Jesus assures us that he is rooted in truth, in eternity, and in relationship with God the Father.

There were harsh punishments for Satan, the beast, and the false prophets throughout this prophecy. Verse 18 warns anyone who adds anything to the prophecy as delivered to John. God will add to that person the plagues described in the prophecy. An even worse consequence is promised to anyone who removes any words from the prophecy. God will remove that person's share in the tree of life and in the holy city.

Upon Jesus declaring, "Yes, I am coming soon!" John writes, "Amen! Come, Lord Jesus!" John is ready. He is prepared to see Jesus again, and he signifies his agreement with the shout of "Amen!"

The final verse of Revelation is verse 21: "The grace of the Lord Jesus be with God's people. Amen." With so much growth needed by the seven churches and all of us living after them, John is right in asking for grace from the Lord Jesus. We have been promised that he is coming again soon; now we need to prepare ourselves by repenting of sin and remaining faithful to Jesus. We want our names to be recorded in the Lamb's Book of Life, and we want that no one be thrown into the fiery lake of burning sulfur forever. Not only do we need to purify our souls, we also need to give the testimony of Jesus Christ to others.

Concerning the nature and identity of God, this last chapter speaks of God and Jesus existing in the city, the new Jerusalem, with their servants. The servants will see "his" face and "his name" will be on their foreheads. It appears that God and Jesus are one in name and locality in this verse.

> ***The throne of God** and of **the Lamb will be in the city**, and his servants will serve him. 4 They will see his face, and **his name will be on their foreheads.***
> —Revelation 22:-3

The Lord God inspires, sends, and shows the future. He inspires his prophets to speak prophecy given by him, and he sends his angels as messengers. His purpose for this is to show the future to those who serve him.

> *"**The Lord, the God** who **inspires the prophets, sent his angel** to **show his servants the things that must soon take place.**"*—Revelation 22:6

In the closing words of Revelation, Jesus once again identifies himself to John, saying that he is coming soon with his reward and judgment for each person for their deeds. We have already read that each person will be rewarded for remaining faithful to the word of God and to the testimony of Jesus Christ. Jesus describes himself as the Alpha and Omega, First and Last, the Beginning and the End. Jesus literally has the first and last words of this prophecy by his authority and identity. He tells John to look, that is, to be aware and ever vigilant for Jesus' second coming.

Again, in verse 16, Jesus identifies himself and declares that he has sent the angel to give this testimony or prophecy to the churches. Jesus describes himself as the root and offspring of David. He is the first, last, and brightest in the Davidic bloodline. He is also the new and final beginning as the bright Morning Star in the new Jerusalem for eternity.

> *"Look, I am coming soon! My reward is with me, and I will give to each person according to what they have done. I am the Alpha and the Omega, the First and the Last, the Beginning and the End.*—Revelation 22:12-13

> *"I, Jesus, have sent my angel to give you this testimony for the churches. I am the Root and the Offspring of David, and the bright Morning Star."* —Revelation 22:16

The last words of Jesus quoted in this prophecy is his reassurance of all that has been promised. God is who he says he is. He does what he said he will do. His word is true.

> *He who testifies to these things says, "Yes, I am coming soon."*—Revelation 22:20

The book of Revelation is a prophecy of hope, of promise, of the ongoing covenant between God and his people. It is a prophetic word of victory over sin, death, Satan, the beast, and false prophets. Revelation is a reminder to live righteously and to refrain from idolatry, immorality, lies, and all sin. It is also a panoramic view of the magnitude of praise to God around this heavenly throne by the angels, saints, prophets, elders, and all living beings.

Praise

Hope

Victory

Covenant

Eternal life

Through our Lord, Jesus Christ, who is coming soon!

Amen!

Reflection

1. Reflecting on the word "soon", how much time do I need to make changes for righteous living?

2. Can I afford to test time by not repenting immediately?

3. When I am challenged in life to make poor decisions, how can this prophecy guide me to make better choices?

4. What questions do I still have about this prophecy?

5. Do I believe this prophecy? What more do I need to do to better understand this message to God's people?

CLOSING THOUGHTS: GOD'S PROMISE OF SALVATION IS FOR EVERYONE!

God created all people and wants to be in a covenant relationship with all people. His law of creation governed the earth until Adam and Eve sinned. Then God put new laws into place to guide his people. Through the laws given to Moses, people were guided to maintain their faith and to love and honor God. Under Mosaic law, the Jewish religion became more focused on the law and less on the meaning behind the law. In the New Testament, the Jewish priests and Pharisees claimed to follow the law of Moses as they awaited the Messiah. However, they did not understand the good news that Jesus came professing for all in the kingdom of God, that the Messiah had come.

> *"One day as Jesus was teaching the people in the temple courts and proclaiming the good news, the chief priests and the teachers of the law, together with the elders, came up to him. 2 "Tell us by what authority you are doing these things," they said. "Who gave you this authority?"*—Luke 20:1-2

Both Peter and Paul learned that the Gospel was meant for all people. When the Holy Spirit fell on both Jews and Gentiles, Peter baptized all who received the Spirit.

> *While Peter was still speaking these words, the Holy Spirit came on all who heard the message. The circumcised believers who had come with Peter were astonished that the gift of the Holy Spirit had been poured out even on Gentiles. For they heard them speaking in tongues and praising God.*
>
> *Then Peter said, "Surely no one can stand in the way of their being baptized with water. They have received the Holy Spirit just as we have."* —Acts 10:44-47

Paul, once a persecutor of Christians, became an apostle for Jesus to both Jews and Gentiles.

> *For I am not ashamed of the gospel, because it is the power of God that brings salvation to everyone who believes: first to the Jew, then to the Gentile.* —Romans 1:16

The book of Revelation declares that the souls of all people were purchased by God through Jesus shedding his blood for our sin. Jesus died for all people, regardless of nation or language. Salvation is for all who believe in Jesus, and we will see people from all nations and languages surrounding the throne of God in heaven. God shows no preferences toward particular skin colors, geographics, cultures, languages, governments, or tribes in heaven. All are our brothers and sisters in Christ, for those who are in Christ. Unity, inclusion of all believers, and access to salvation are emphasized in the book of Revelation. In Revelation 3:20, Jesus makes it clear that he stands ready and waiting for everyone to hear his voice and dine with him at his table.

Revelation 3:20 Here I am! I stand at the door and knock. If anyone hears my voice and opens the door, I will come in and eat with that person, and they with me.

Revelation 5:9 And they sang a new song, saying: "You are worthy to take the scroll and to open its seals, because you were slain, and with your blood you purchased for God persons from every tribe and language and people and nation.

Revelation 7:9 After this I looked, and there before me was a great multitude that no one could count, from every nation, tribe, people and language, standing before the throne and before the Lamb. They were wearing white robes and were holding palm branches in their hands.

Revelation 10:11 Then I was told, "You must prophesy again about many peoples, nations, languages and kings."

Revelation 11:9 For three and a half days some from every people, tribe, language and nation will gaze on their bodies and refuse them burial.

Revelation 13:7 It was given power to wage war against God's holy people and to conquer them. And it was given authority over every tribe, people, language and nation.

Revelation 14:6 Then I saw another angel flying in midair, and he had the eternal gospel to proclaim to those who live on the earth—to every nation, tribe, language and people.

Revelation 15:4 Who will not fear you, Lord, and bring glory to your name? For you alone are holy. All nations will come and worship before you, for your righteous acts have been revealed."

Revelation 17:15 Then the angel said to me, "The waters you saw, where the prostitute sits, are peoples, multitudes, nations and languages.

Revelation 22:2 On each side of the river stood the tree of life, bearing twelve crops of fruit, yielding its fruit every month. And the leaves of the tree are for the healing of the nations.

In case you have read the book of Revelation and wondered if heaven is meant for you, if you needed to do anything to earn eternal life with God in heaven, if Jesus died on the cross for you, if God wants to be in a covenant relationship with you, the answer is unequivocally YES! No one can exclude you from God and salvation through his son, Jesus Christ, except you, if you exclude yourself from God! Then you will be judged according to your deeds: Did you or did you not stay faithful to the word of God and to the testimony of Jesus Christ? Beyond that, regardless of your nation, tribe, language,or current state of spirituality, God sent Jesus to earth to die for you and for all of our sin so that you and all believers would spend eternity with the Triune God: Father, Son, and Holy Spirit. Doesn't that sound better than wondering where we came from or where we are going? Doesn't clarity for your future sound better than confusion and chaos?

In Matthew 18, Jesus teaches God's love for us in the form of this parable.

> *"What do you think? If a man owns a hundred sheep, and one of them wanders away, will he not leave the ninety-nine on the hills and go to look for the one that wandered off? And if he finds it, truly I tell you, he is happier about that one sheep than about the ninety-nine that did not wander off. In the same way your Father in heaven is not willing that any of these little ones should perish.*—Matthew 18:12-14

Closing Prayer

Lord God,

We give you all the praise, honor, and glory for who you are. You are the Alpha and Omega, the First and the Last. We praise you for your powerful yet gentle Holy Spirit.

We thank you for your Son, Jesus Christ, who died on the cross to save us from our sins and sinful natures. We are in awe of your everlasting grace and mercy, your compassion on us, your enduring patience toward the saved and unsaved.

We want to join the angels and saints in praising you around your throne in heaven, and we seek to lead a righteous life toward that end of spending eternity with you.

We thank you for your holy Word that speaks truth and faithfulness. We honor you for your eternal covenant to be our God and for us to be your people.

Come and dwell within our hearts and purify our souls so that we can be unified in your spirit and love.

We are forever grateful that you have created us, that you have instructed us, and that you have guided us to live each day with eyes to see, ears to hear, and hearts to feel your majesty, mercy, and greatness.

There is no one like you. May you be glorified and honored by all that we say and do. May we be made whole and holy in your sight! Until Jesus comes again, we say and sing, "Hallelujah! Amen! Come, Lord Jesus. Come!"

For Further Study

For Further Study in Revelation

Most everyone needs to read the book of Revelation more than once to understand all the levels of meanings, symbolism, themes, and truths about God. Here are some recurring themes for you to think about as you continue your study of this amazing prophetic revelation as recorded by John.

1. The character and identity of God: Father, Son, and Spirit
2. The character and identity of Satan (the devil)
3. Victory in Jesus: promises for the victorious
4. Praise and worship
5. The sounds in Revelation
6. God's word and the testimony of Jesus Christ
7. God's covenant with his people
8. Salvation for every people, tribe, language, and nation

REVELATION CHART OF SPIRITUAL BEINGS BY CHAPTER

		JESUS CHRIST		GOD		SPIRIT		ANGELS
Chapter 1							1:1	Sending his angel to his servant John
			1:4	Who is and was and is to come	1:4	From the seven spirits before his throne		
	1:5	faithful witness						
	1:5	first born of the dead						
	1:5	ruler of the kings of the earth						
	1:5	To him who loves us and has freed us from our sins by his blood,						

	1:6	him who) has made us to be a kingdom and priests to serve his God and Father						
			1:8	I am the Alpha and the Omega,"				
			1:8	who is, and who was, and who is to come, the Almighty				
					1:10	I was in the Spirit		
	1:13	son of man						
	1:17							
	1:18	the living one						
							1:20	The seven stars are the angels of the seven churches

		JESUS CHRIST		GOD		SPIRIT		ANGELS
Chapter 2	2:1	him who holds the seven stars in his right hand and walks among the seven golden lampstands						
					2:7	hear what the Spirit says to the churches		
	2:8	First and the Last, who died and came to life again					2:8	To the angel of the church in Smyrna
					2:11	Spirit says to the churches		
	2:12	him who has the sharp, double-edged sword						
					2:17	Spirit says to the churches		
	2:18	Son of God					2:18	To the angel of the church in Thyatira
					2:29	Spirit says to the churches		

Chapter 3	3:1	him who holds the seven spirits of God and the seven stars			3:1	seven spirits of God	3:1	To the angel of the church in Sardis
							3:5	Before my Father and his angels
					3:6	Spirit says to the churches		
	3:7	him who is holy and true, who holds the kdy of David					3:7	To the angel of the church in Philadelphia
	3:10	protector from the hour of trial						
	3:12	knowledge of new name of God						
					3:13	Spirit says to the churches		
	3:14	Amen, the faithful and true witness, the ruler of God's creation					3:14	To the angel of the church in Laodicea
					3:22	Spirit says to the churches		

		JESUS CHRIST		GOD		SPIRIT		ANGELS
Chapter 4	2:1				4:2	I was in the Spirit		
					4:57	seven spirits of God		
			4:8	"Holy, holy, holy is the Lord God Almighty. who was, and is, and is to come.				
			4:11	worthy, our Lord and God, to receive glory and honor and power				
Chapter 5			5:1	sat on the throne				
	5:5	the Lion of the tribe of Judah, the root of David						
	5:6	Lamb			5:6	seven spirits of God sent out into all the earth		

	5:9-10	worthy to take the scrolls, blood purchased for God the people, made them a priesthood and kingdom						
							5:11	voice of many angels, numbering thousands upon thousands, and ten thousand times ten thousand
	5:12	"Worthy is the Lamb, who was slain, to receive power and wealth and wisdom and strength and honor and glory and praise!						
	5:13	Lamb	5:13	To him who sits on the throne				

		JESUS CHRIST		GOD		SPIRIT		ANGELS
Chapter 6	6:1	Lamb			4:2	I was in the Spirit		
	6:10	Sovereign Lord, holy and true	6:9-10	Sovereign Lord, holy and true, avenger	4:57	seven spirits of God		
	6:16	wrath of the Lamb	6:16	sits on the throne				
Chapter 7							7:1	four angels standing at the four corners of the earth
			7:2	the living God			7:2	four angels who had been given power to harm the land and the sea
	7:10	Lamb	7:10	our God, who sits on the throne				
							7:11	All the angels were standing around the throne
			7:15	he who sits on the throne				
	7:17	Lamb at the center of the throne will be their shepherd	7:17	God				

Chapter 8	8:2	God					8:2	seven angels who stand before God
							8:3	angel, who had a golden censer
							8:4	The smoke of the incense, together with the prayers of God's people, went up before God from the angel's hand
							8:5	angel took the censer
							8:6	seven angels who had the seven trumpets
							8:7	he first angel sounded his trumpet,
							8:8	The second angel sounded his trumpet
							3:14	To the angel of the church in Laodicea

		JESUS CHRIST		GOD		SPIRIT		ANGELS
Chapter 9							9:1	The fifth angel sounded his trumpet
							9:11	angel of the Abyss
							9:13	The sixth angel sounded his trumpet
							9:14	Release the four angels who are bound at the great river Euphrates
							9:15	the four angels who had been kept ready for this very hour and day and month and year
Chapter 10							10:1	another mighty angel

							10:5	Then the angel I had seen standing on the sea and on the land raised his right hand to heaven.
							10:7	seventh angel is about to sound his trumpet
	10:8	voice that I had heard from heaven					10:8	the scroll that lies open in the hand of the angel
							10:9-10	I went to the angel and asked him to give me the little scroll
Chapter 11	11:15	Messiah	11:15	Our Lord			11:15	The seventh angel sounded his trumpet
			11:17	Lord God Almighty, the One who is and who was				

		JESUS CHRIST		GOD		SPIRIT		ANGELS
Chapter 12							12:1	Michael and his angels fought against the dragon
							12:9	He was hurled to the earth, and his angels with him
	12:10	Messiah	12:10	Our God				
	12:11	Lamb						
	12:17	Jesus	12:17	God				
Chapter 13	13:8	Lamb who was slain from the creation of the world.						
Chapter 14	14:1	Lamb	14:1	His Father				
							14:6	angel flying in midair, and he had the eternal gospel to proclaim to those who live on the earth—to every nation, tribe, language and people

			14:7	him who made the heavens, the earth, the sea and the springs of water				
							14:8	A second angel followed
							14:9	A second angel followed
							14:10	in the presence of the holy angels
							14:13	"Yes," says the Spirit, "they will rest from their labor, for their deeds will follow them."
	14;14	son of man with a crown of gold on his head and a sharp sickle in his hand						

		JESUS CHRIST		GOD		SPIRIT		ANGELS
							14:15	son of man with a crown of gold on his head and a sharp sickle in his hand
	14:16	he who was seated on the cloud						
							14:17	Another angel came out of the temple in heaven
							14:18	Still another angel, who had charge of the fire
							14:19	The angel swung his sickle on the earth
Chapter 15							15:1	seven angels with the seven last plagues
			15:3-4	great, marvelous, Lord God Almighty, just true, King of the Nations, holy, righteous				

							15:6	seven angels with the seven plagues
							15:7	seven angels seven golden bowls filled with the wrath of God
							15:8	seven plagues of the seven angels
Chapter 16							16:1	seven angels
							16:2	The first angel went and poured out his bowl on the land
							16:3	The second angel poured out his bowl on the sea
							16:4	The third angel poured out his bowl on the rivers
			16:5	You are just in these judgments, O Holy One, you who are and who were			16:5	I heard the angel in charge of the waters

		JESUS CHRIST		GOD		SPIRIT		ANGELS
			16:7	Lord God Almighty, true and just				
							16:8	The fourth angel poured out his bowl on the sun
							16:10	The fifth angel poured out his bowl on the throne of the beast,
			16:11	God of heaven				
							16:12	The sixth angel poured out his bowl on the great river Euphrates
			16:14	God Almighty				
							16:17	The seventh angel poured out his bowl into the air
			16:19	God remembered and gave fury of his wrath				

Chapter 17							17:1	One of the seven angels
					17:3	angel carried me away in the Spirit	17:3	angel carried me away in the Spirit
							17:7	Then the angel said to me: "Why are you astonished?
	17:14	Lord of lords and King of kings						
							17:15	Then the angel said to me,
Chapter 18							18:1	I saw another angel coming down from heaven
			18:8	mighty is the Lord God who judges				
			18:20	God Judges				
							18:21	Then a mighty angel picked up a boulder

		JESUS CHRIST		GOD		SPIRIT		ANGELS
Chapter 19			19:1-2	our God, for true and just are his judgments				
			19:6	Lord God Almighty				
	19:7	Lamb						
							19:9	Then the angel said to me, "Write this
					19:10	For it is the Spirit of prophecy who bears testimony to Jesus		
	19:11	rider is called Faithful and True						
			19:15	God Almighty				
	19:16	king of kings and lord of lords.						
							19:17	I saw an angel standing in the sun

Chapter 20							20:1	saw an angel coming down out of heaven, having the key to the Abyss and holding in his hand a great chain
	20:4	Christ						
Chapter 21			21:3	God dwells with his people				
			21:5	He who was seated on the throne				
			21:6	I am the Alpha and the Omega, the Beginning and the End				
			21:7	God as Father "they will be my people"				
							21:9	One of the seven angels
					21:10	he carried me away in the Spirit		

		JESUS CHRIST		GOD		SPIRIT		ANGELS
Chapter 21							21:12	twelve angels at the gates
							21:15	The angel who talked with me had a measuring rod of gold to measure the city, its gates and its walls
							21:17	The angel measured the wall
	21:22	Lamb	21:22	Lord God Almighty				
Chapter 22	22:1	Lamb	22:1	God				
			22:5	Lord God				

			22:6	Lord, the God who inspires the prophets			22:6	The angel said to me, "These words are trustworthy and true. The Lord, the God who inspires the prophets, sent his angel to show his servants the things that must soon take place."
	22:13	I am the Alpha and the Omega, the First and the Last, the Beginning and the End.						
	22:16	I, Jesus...I am the Root and the Offspring of David, and the bright Morning Star						
					22:17	The Spirit and the bride say, "Come!"		
	22:20	Lord Jesus						
	22:21	Lord Jesus						

AFTERWORD

AFTERWORD

Like many or most of you, I have had a complex relationship with Revelation. I call it a relationship because to me all of Scripture is a living, moving, breathing thing. To be honest, I didn't really read the entire book all the way through with serious consideration until I was well into my Fuller Seminary education. I had driven out to Saint Andrew's Abbey in Valyermo, California, one day for a spiritual retreat with the sole purpose of reading Revelation in one sitting. It was a beautiful day. I remember sitting in a deck chair in a wooded area with the sun dappling through the trees, quietly noticing other retreatants as they passed by in silence. I took it slow and steady, one chapter at a time, making a mental note to never preach from this book unless I was in a life threatening or kidnapped type of true-crime situation. I say that with a grain of humorous salt...of course, we preach what is asked of us by the Holy Spirit...but Revelation is so weird. And complex. And scary. And glorious. Crafting a sermon from the words of John the Revelator daunted me. It still does.

Fast forward to my first call in 1998 as an Associate Pastor at Eastland Church of God in Lexington, Kentucky. I had been there for two years and had been asked to come back and teach in the Religious Studies department at my alma mater, Anderson University, in Indiana. At my church's "going away" party for me, an art teacher at the church presented me with an enormous silk painting of St. Matthew from the Book of Kells specifically referenced from Revelation 4:6-8.

> *...Around the throne and on each side of the throne, are four living creatures...the third living creature with a face like a human...Day and night without ceasing they sing, "Holy, holy, holy, the Lord God the Almighty, who was and is and is to come."*

The art teacher's husband had made a lovely etched frame. This painting has moved wherever I have moved...from Indiana to Vermont to Pennsylvania to Los Angeles to Ohio, always above my fireplace. If my house burned down, it would be the possession I would race to save. I also long to be a creature who never ceases singing the praises of God.

Fast forward again to my life in ministry, where I have officiated hundreds of funerals, almost always quoting about a "New Jerusalem" and that our salty and painful tears will be wiped away "there" and that there is a place beyond this place. A place of peace and hope and fulfillment. With God. And dogs.

And now my lovely friend has written an inspired book to add to the continued conversation about Revelation. I first saw Nancy Hulshult in the mid-1980s when I was a teenager during a Sunday morning church service. I remember looking to my right in the pew behind me, where there was a new woman with three young boys sitting there, and someone told me that she was a gymnastics judge and worked at our church school. It was years later before we would ever really speak, but my life hasn't been the same since. She is the Naomi to my Ruth and a mentor to many. She doesn't have to use words (even though she has plenty, HA!) to speak or serve. From her admired work in education to earning her doctorate and becoming an ordained minister, Nancy always knows how to keep it real, and joy follows her. And in retirement, she has become a prolific writer!

Since you are reading the Afterword, it is assumed you have read or at least skimmed the book. Nancy has put forth a thorough and thoughtful layout of God's revelation to John on Patmos. First and foremost, Nancy always points us to the praise, all the while adding thoughtful commentary and reflection questions along the way. Nancy never demands the reader agree with her but rather prompts us to practice critical thinking inspired by the Holy Spirit to come to our own personal conclusions. Revelation is not touchy-feely or a warm hug. Instead, Revelation is direct, graphic and sometimes harsh. Nancy helps us to read between the lines and see God at work in the place prepared for each of us who believe.

I end with a quote from another Church of God female minister and teacher, Dr. Marie Strong (d.1995). Dr. Strong served as a Bible Professor for 28 years at Anderson College/University, Indiana. In 1980, she published a small book entitled, "Basic Teachings from Patmos". She writes in her first chapter, "The Book of Revelation seems very different from other biblical books. It is a book full of angels doing strange things, of beasts, of dragons, of the earth opening its mouth and swallowing rivers. Living creatures speak and horses of varied colors gallop across the pages of history. What is the meaning of this peculiar book, or does it have a meaning? Is it, as one scholar has suggested, the wild ravings of the mad man from Patmos? Why is such a strange book in the Bible? What meaning could it possibly have for us?"

Nancy has added her name to the long list of brave authors to face Revelation with respect and awe. What meaning does this book and Revelation have for you?

Maybe take some time to sit in a chair in the sun and reflect, or look at a great painting, or really pay attention at your next funeral you attend... because the Revelation continues. May we all sing loudly together, "Holy, Holy, Holy!"

Thank you, Nancy.

Respectfully submitted,
Rev. Amy L. Arnold, MDiv.
July 2024

APPENDIX A

TESTIMONIES

FROM 2024 TRENTON GRACEPOINTE NAZARENE CHURCH

WOMEN'S RETREAT: "JOURNEY TOGETHER"

HUESTON WOODS LODGE

OXFORD, OHIO

Testimony by Cheryl Young

Each year as Women's Retreat planning begins, prayer is at the center of what plans are made. As the Women's Ministry Director, I know our women pretty well; seven years of planning retreats for them has given me insight. But I don't know them as well as their Heavenly Father, who created them, so I need His prompting and leading. I had some ideas rolling around in my head and heart when I met with Nancy about being our speaker but was open to what God was speaking to her about what to share with us.

I was a bit surprised when she mentioned the book of Revelation for our theme. So often we think of this book as confusing, scary, almost depressing. Almost like it's only there for pastors and Bible scholars to read and understand. Yet, as she began to share what God was speaking into her heart I knew that this was what He wanted – so Revelation it was! Digging into this last book of the Bible in preparation for the retreat, I was reminded that this is a book of victory and praise!

I love stories that end in "happily ever after." On hard days I've been known to binge watch Hallmark movies for that very reason. When reading a book, I've been known to peek at the ending to make sure I want to keep reading the book. Even though there are characters such as Satan, the Anti-Christ and the false prophet and the plot speaks of war and martyrs, the book of Revelation is our happily ever after! Preparing for the Prayer Walk of Praise that was to take place during the retreat, my main focus on the entire book was the prayers of praise proclaimed around the throne for Christ, the One, who is victorious!

My husband is currently battling prostate cancer. We spent most of the weeks leading up to our Women's Retreat up in Columbus where he was receiving treatment. There were hard days and yet, as I focused on the praises of the saints in Revelation I was reminded that "God himself will be with them. He will wipe every tear from their eyes and there will be no more death or sorrow or crying or pain." (Rev. 21:3-4). I'm reminded of the line in the Shane and Shane song that says "I know how the story ends! We will be with you again!" Oh, the hope we have in the hard times! This is temporary – victory awaits us!! The book of Revelation has been such encouragement, even when times are hard. Praise His name!

Cheryl Young
Women's Director
GracePointe Nazarene Church

Testimony by Karin Bowman

I didn't think that I really had anything to share about the retreat. But when Cheryl mentioned writing our testimony again at Bible study, God just said, "What about yours, Karin?" and I had to stop and think about what in the world I would have to say. Then I knew.

Nancy asked us to go to the back of the room and choose a case. I went back and looked for number 24 (birthday for my husband and for me), and it was gone...so I picked up another. I watched as the other girls at my table and around me opened their cases and found treasures and counted money...and I opened mine to find....Hamburger Helper. Hamburger Helper?!?!? No money. No treasure. I was so caught up in my disappointment....I almost missed the point that day...and could have still been missing it, if God hadn't moved on my heart to look closer.

Thankfully, my friend, Michelle, told me to "read your verse!"....and there it was in Revelation..."If anyone hears My voice and opens the door, I will come in and eat with that person, and they with Me." Wait!? What just happened? I got zero money. I didn't get a mask with sequins or a fascinator...but didn't I just get the most amazing gift? DINNER WITH JESUS!!! Reflecting on it now...weeks later, it is humbling. I was so caught up in what the rest of the world had going on, I didn't fully appreciate the greatest gift I was given.
It has struck me, while reflecting on this now, how often we live our lives that way...too caught up in the comparison and looking at what everyone has or is doing, even how others are blessed with the very things that are my own heart's desire. I'm just so human.

What I realize now is that I am not going to change overnight. I am still human and likely will find myself comparing to others again and again, but I hope when I do that, when I am reflecting on the "me, me, me" instead of "God, God, God" that He will have the grace to remind me that sometimes the greatest give we can be given is a box of Hamburger Helper.
by Karin "Cheeseburger Macaroni" Bowman :)

> *Those whom I love I rebuke and discipline. So be earnest and repent. Here I am! I stand at the door and knock. If anyone hears my voice and opens the door, I will come in and eat with that person, and they with me. To the one who is victorious, I will give the right to sit with me on my throne, just as I was victorious and sat down with my Father on his throne.* —Revelation 3:19-21

Testimony by Courtney Whitlock

My testimony started the moment I got married to my amazing husband. We got married young and knew instantly that we wanted to be parents. We tried for years and went through two miscarriages before we decided to see a fertility specialist. He helped us so much throughout our journey, and we were blessed to become pregnant with our first IUI fertility treatment. Unfortunately, that pregnancy resulted in our third miscarriage. We went through another IUI that was unsuccessful and at that point, after eight years of trying to have a baby. I was starting to really struggle with my faith. I'd cry out to God just about every night, asking him to show me a sign, to tell me whether I needed to start accepting the fact that I was just not meant to be a mother, or if I just needed to continue to be patient. But every time I prayed, nothing in my heart changed. I still felt that I was meant to be a mom.

The time came for our third IUI treatment. We weren't sure if we were going to be able to afford this last treatment, but our amazing church at the time raised money to pay for another IUI. I had told myself, "Okay, God provided for another treatment. If this one doesn't work, then I am taking a break." But by the grace of God this was the IUI that provided my husband and I with our amazing son.

Now fast forward six years, my husband and I started attending a new church. A friend told me about a women's retreat for the church that she would love me to go to, so on the last day to register, I signed up. During this retreat we played a game of "Deal or No Deal". We were to pick a number and go get the box with that number on it. I had originally decided that I was going to pick the number 24 for my son's birthday, but when I got up there, 24 was gone, so I decided on 14 for my husband's birthday. I opened the box, and there were name tags with a bible verse. The bible verse was Revelation 3:7-13. I instantly cried when I saw the contents of the box and read the verse. The verse talked about God simply shutting a door that you want open. The verse encouraged faith in spite of difficult circumstances, faith when you feel your weakest. Also, something nobody knew except for my husband and me: when I found out the gender of our miracle baby, I told my husband by putting a onesie inside a box with our future son's name on a name tag that read, "Hello my name is Andrew".

The day I shared this testimony with my new church (the day after the retreat) was also the anniversary of my son being dedicated to God during a service at church. I hadn't felt that close to God since the moment I found out I was pregnant with my son. I knew in that moment that God was telling me again, that he was holding doors open for me and that he would close the doors that needed to be closed.

The Faithful Church

"And to the angel of the church in Philadelphia write,

'These things says He who is holy, He who is true, "He who has the key of David, He who opens and no one shuts, and shuts and no one opens": "I know your works. See, I have set before you an open door, and no one can shut it; for you have a little strength, have kept My word, and have not denied My name. Indeed I will make those of the synagogue of Satan, who say they are Jews and are not, but lie—indeed I will make them come and worship before your feet, and to know that I have loved you. Because you have kept My command to persevere, I also will keep you from the hour of trial which shall come upon the whole world, to test those who dwell on the earth. Behold, I am coming quickly! Hold fast what you have, that no one may take your crown. He who overcomes, I will make him a pillar in the temple of My God, and he shall go out no more. I will write on him the name of My God and the name of the city of My God, the New Jerusalem, which comes down out of heaven from My God. And I will write on him My new name.

"He who has an ear, let him hear what the Spirit says to the churches."'—Revelation 3:7-13

Testimony by Shari Miller

The book of Revelation may not be the first book of the Bible that one would choose for devotional reading. As a matter of fact, it used to be my last choice. In the past, many speakers used Revelation as a fearsome and scary sermon series on end times. Nancy has changed my perspective from scary to joyful. The book of Revelation allows us to peek behind the veil of heaven. It allows us to see the overwhelming love of God, the magnitude of His glory,the praise that fills the Heavens, the angels that worship, the beauty of His promises, and splendor of the streets of gold. Oh, what a day that will be, to be is His presence. I have been so encouraged, uplifted and feel like I walk a bit closer with my Savior. Thank you, Nancy, for sharing the book of Revelation and prompting us to go deeper with Him.

Testimony by Rebecca Craft

It was a bitterly cold Saturday morning in January. My son had flown back to San Diego; both of my daughters had returned to their respective schools for the new semester; my husband was working; and I was home. Alone. The bustle of the holidays had ceased as suddenly as an unwound clock. My feelings matched the view from my kitchen window above the sink: cold, barren, and bleak. A deep sense of sadness was growing in the pit of my stomach, and I felt the familiar anxiety start in my chest and move up toward the lump in my throat. I laid my phone down, said, "Alexa, play praise and worship music", and picked up a broom as music began to fill the room.

As I began cleaning and singing, God started speaking to me about the women's retreat. It hadn't been on my mind and was a welcome distraction from the sadness and anxiety.

"What songs should we sing, Lord?"

"Just worship me."

"But I want to make sure we sing the perfect songs to fit whatever the theme will be, and also draw people closer to you."

"Just worship me."

"But God, I - ..."

"Just worship me, Daughter. I'll be there."

Then words began speaking into a deep place in me, resonating with a peaceful stillness. I grabbed my phone to write them down.

"There will be Sisters that come to the retreat that have experienced so much change. Some will be joyful changes that came through new family, new jobs, new experiences. Some Sisters will have endured losses so deep that they can't speak of them without weeping. In every addition and subtraction, I am there. I am the Alpha and the Omega. The Beginning and the End. Worship me. I will be there."

I realized that the sadness had lifted, and the anxiety had dissipated. For the days, weeks, and months that followed, the words "Just worship me" continued to echo in me.

At the retreat planning meeting with the team and Nancy, she presented her talking points for the retreat. "The teachings are going to be from Revelation. I would like us to do a Worship Walk." Then she handed out laminated cards that contained scripture from Revelation, all verses of praise and worship:

Holy, holy, holy
Is the Lord God Almighty,
Who was, and is, and is to come.
—Revelation 4:8

You are worthy, our Lord and God,
to receive glory and honor and power,
for you created all things,
and by your will they were created
and have their being.
—Revelation 4:11

Worthy is the Lamb, who was slain,
to receive power and wealth,
and wisdom and strength
and honor and glory and praise!
—Revelation 4:12

To Him who sits on the throne
and to the Lamb
be praise and honor and glory and power
forever and ever!
—Revelation 4:13

Amen!
Praise and glory
and wisdom and thanks
and honor and power and strength
be to our God for ever and ever.
Amen!
—Revelation 7:12

I stared at the card, amazed at the perfection of God. Worship Walk? Verses exclusively of praise and worship? The symmetry of His plan for the retreat was evident, even though none of us had spoken with each other about what we were receiving from Him in preparation.

Over the next few months, my husband and I unexpectedly walked through changes impacting some of those we love most in this world: divorce, depression, alcoholism, a new job. I'd like to say I handled it with grace and spiritual maturity, but mostly I ended up with skinned knees from falling down: sometimes to pray, sometimes to yell and shake my fist in anger. By the time the Retreat weekend rolled around, I felt like I limped in the door, bruised, abraded and lacerated by life.

But oh, HE WAS THERE.

Nancy taught us about discarding our baggage, relinquishing our human identifying labels, and becoming God's servants; to put on the armor of God, and to accept His reward for us.

In one of the applications of the teaching, dozens upon dozens of scrolls containing scripture were on a table in the back of the room. Each one was different. We were told to randomly pick up one and return to our seats. Tears, gasps, and laughter began popping up from each of the tables as we began to open and read our scrolls. Although "randomly" selected, God had supernaturally made each person's scroll speak directly to them. Of course, mine was about worship!

> *Then I heard what sounded like a great multitude,*
> *like the roar of rushing waters*
> *and like loud peals of thunder, shouting:*
> *"Hallelujah! For our Lord God Almighty reigns"*
> *Let us rejoice and be glad and give him glory!*
> *For the wedding of the lamb has come,*
> *and his bride has made herself ready.*
> —Revelation 19:6-7

Worship shows up in the Bible from Genesis to Revelation. Psalm 18 says it saves us from our enemies and that He hears our voice in His temple. Worship helps us let go, submitting to Him as we shed our old selves and embrace the transformative power of God. Worship acknowledges His goodness and greatness and glory, helping us to bend our knees and bow our heads in humility and reverence, giving Him the place as King over our lives. Worship fills our mind, casting out the anxiety that cripples us, and allows us to finish the race with long, strong strides. Worship heals us in those quiet moments when, our hearts and minds full of Him, He is able to speak into us and share His peace and plan. Worship paradoxically prepares us to rise up for a mighty battle against our adversaries, and yet softens our hearts in service toward the weak. the least of these.

I walked into a Celebrate Recovery meeting recently in support of a loved one. I sat with my arms crossed during worship, trying to understand how things had come to this. But the worship music broke through my intrusive thoughts, and He began to speak to me.

A week later, I walked back into Celebrate Recovery. God had opened my eyes to things the week before during worship that I needed to submit to Him and be healed from, including codependency and anxiety. The last worship song was Big Daddy Weave's "Redeemed." As the words began to sink in, I lifted my hands when the words of the bridge started:

Because I don't have to be
the old man inside of me
'cause his day is long dead and gone
Because I've got a new name
A new life - I'm not the same
and a Hope that will carry me home

As the chorus started, the tears fell and the weight lifted from my shoulders:

I am redeemed
You set me free
So I'll shake off these heavy chains
and wipe away every stain
'Cause I'm not who I used to be
'Cause I am redeemed
Thank God redeemed

In that moment, gripped by the message of the lyrics, fully engulfed in praise to my loving Father, and feeling lighter than I had in so long, His words came back to me so swiftly: "Just worship me, Daughter. I'll be there."

And He is.

Appendix B

"Journey Together": A Retreat Plan

Knowing, Loving, and Serving God

SESSION ONE: THE OLD SUITCASE

(Freedom to be a kingdom of priests who **serve** God)

Activity: "Unpacking" the unnecessary and irrelevant from your suitcase of life:

1. diaper bag of your DNA/genetics
2. backpack of your environment from preschool through college
3. carry-on of marriage and/or career.

What needs to be discarded from your "baggage" in order to be fully free, fully identifying as a priest, fully serving God and not man or the flesh? We travel through life in this world and the next as a COMMUNITY, a great multitude of believers, for God loves US and has freed US and has made US to serve Him only. "Worship God!" (Rev. 19:10 and Rev. 22:9)

Revelation 1:5b-6 (US)

To him who loves us and has freed us from our sins by his blood, and has made us to be a kingdom and priests to serve his God and Father—to him be glory and power for ever and ever! Amen.

Revelation 7:9 (COMMUNITY OF BELIEVERS)

After this I looked, and there before me was a great multitude that no one could count, from every nation, tribe, people and language, standing before the throne and before the Lamb.

Let's look at the 7 Churches for a time of self-reflection: with whom do we most identify?

SESSION TWO: THE BELT BAG (Belt of Truth to know God) & SCROLLS

No seal on Scripture for us!

Activity: Prayer Walk of Praise - praising God, listening for truth from God to know Him better and to know us better. Each person receives an individualized scroll with a verse from Revelation for reflection and discussion. In each Belt Bag is a laminated "Pocket Praise" card with praise songs from Revelation. What do we need to carry with us in order to pray and praise him continuously?

Ephesians 6:10-18

Finally, be strong in the Lord and in his mighty power. Put on the full armor of God, so that you can take your stand against the devil's schemes. For our struggle is not against flesh and blood, but against the rulers, against the authorities, against the powers of this dark world and against the spiritual forces of evil in the heavenly realms. Therefore put on the full armor of God, so that when the day of evil comes, you may be able to stand your ground, and after you have done everything, to stand. Stand firm then, with the belt of truth buckled around your waist, with the breastplate of righteousness in place, and with your feet fitted with the readiness that comes from the gospel of peace. In addition to all this, take up the shield of faith, with which you can extinguish all the flaming arrows of the evil one. Take the helmet of salvation and the sword of the Spirit, which is the word of God.

And pray in the Spirit on all occasions with all kinds of prayers and requests. With this in mind, be alert and always keep on praying for all the Lord's people.

Revelation 20:10 Spiritual Warfare against Satan, the Antichrist, and the false prophet are the three adversaries in Revelation (the Dragon, the Beast of the Sea, and the Beast of the Earth).

Revelation 12:7-12 (WHERE IT BEGAN)

Then war broke out in heaven. Michael and his angels fought against the dragon, and the dragon and his angels fought back. 8 But he was not strong enough, and they lost their place in heaven. 9 The great dragon was hurled down—that ancient serpent called the devil, or Satan, who leads the whole world astray. He was hurled to the earth, and his angels with him.

Then I heard a loud voice in heaven say:
"Now have come the salvation and the power
and the kingdom of our God,
and the authority of his Messiah.
For the accuser of our brothers and sisters,
who accuses them before our God day and night,
has been hurled down.

They triumphed over him
by the blood of the Lamb
and by the word of their testimony;
they did not love their lives so much
as to shrink from death.

Therefore rejoice, you heavens
and you who dwell in them!
But woe to the earth and the sea,
because the devil has gone down to you!
He is filled with fury,
because he knows that his time is short.".

Why we need to study the Word, pray, give praise and testimonies: We need to be alert and equipped to see all three adversaries for who they are. We need the belt of truth (the Word of God) to discern the Enemy and false prophets and witnesses. We need to pray to draw strength from the Lord. We need to praise God as our testimonies of faith. We need to know that we are victorious in Christ to the very end, regardless of the strategies of our adversaries. The Holy Trinity of God, Son, and Spirit defeats the trinity of Satan, Beast of the Sea, and the Beast of the Earth.

2/18/2024 the Word from God at the altar:
"My Word, Bible, is your sword/my sword, my shield/your shield...learn how to use it better and faster and clearer and cleaner, then go and fight the dragon in my name, the name I will give you, and in the name of my son, Jesus, with courage, hope, faith, and great joy!!!! Dig in and go, make disciples of all nations!"

12:11 Dragon and accusers defeated by the blood of the Lamb and BY THEIR TESTIMONY and they did not love their lives so much that they were afraid to die.

12:17 and the Dragon was angry at the woman and declared war against the rest of her children-- all who keep God's commandments and MAINTAIN THEIR TESTIMONY FOR JESUS!

Revelation 21:-6-7 (WHERE IT ENDS)

He said to me: "It is done. I am the Alpha and the Omega, the Beginning and the End. To the thirsty I will give water without cost from the spring of the water of life. Those who are victorious will inherit all this, and I will be their God and they will be my children.

From beginning to end, the Bible proclaims God's covenant with us, God's promise to us: "I will be their God and they will be my people."

SESSION THREE: THE CASE FOR TODAY (God's Reward for Us)

Revelation 22:12-14

> *"Look, I am coming soon! My reward is with me, and I will give to each person according to what they have done. I am the Alpha and the Omega, the First and the Last, the Beginning and the End. "Blessed are those who wash their robes, that they may have the right to the tree of life and may go through the gates into the city...".*

Activity: Deal or No Deal Game: In each numbered case there is a verse from Revelation, a symbol from the verse, and bills of assorted denominations of "money". Each participant chooses a case, opens it and reads the verse. Discuss the meaning of the verse and symbol, and calculate who has the most and least money of the group. Participants can trade ONCE with another participant, or entire tables of participants can make ONE group trade. Once all "deals" are made, the phone rings as the "banker" calls in one final deal.

For example, one case had a fake $100 bill, a sample bottle of mouthwash, and the verse from Revelation 3:16, "So, because you are lukewarm—neither hot nor cold—I am about to spit you out of my mouth."

For another example, a case had $1M bill, plastic tiaras, and the verse from Revelation 19:12, "His eyes are like blazing fire, and on his head are many crowns."

The following chart has ideas for up to 60 cases, but others are possible.

Case#	Contents	Verse	Message
1	plush ox	4:7	around the throne singing worship
2	gold star stickers	2:1-7	Repent
3	plastic tiara	2:8-11	Crown of life/Remain faithful
4	handcuffs	2:8-11	devil-prison-test/Don't fear suffering
5	toy ships	8:9	ships of rich destroyed
6	white stone	2:12-17	
7	plastic dental swords	2:12-17	repent of tolerance of false teachings
8	Morning Star	2:18-29	hold tightly to what you have & I give you authority over all nations
9	book of suffering	2:18-29	false prophet Jezebel/Suffering for adultery
10	Book of Life	3:1-6	Name recorded: announce to My Father and his angels: "You are mine"
11	Alarm clock	3:1-6	Wake up; go back to what you first heard and believed
12	Thief (handcuffs)	3:1-6	I will come to you if you don't wake up
13	Pillar (candle)	3:7-13	Protection from great testing
14	Name tags	3:7-13	Persevere! My new name on you
15	Foot cream	3:7-13	Satan's liars bow at Jews' feet
16	Hamburger Helper	3:14-22	Be diligent; turn from indifference
17	Throne/crown	3:14-22	Sit with me on my throne
18	plastic eagle	4:7	around the throne singing worship
19	bottled water	3:14-22	lukewarm
20	toy gold coins	3:14-22	exports "buy from me"
21	Keys	1:9-20	Jesus holds keys to Hades and death
22	1st trumpet (kazoo)	8:7	1st trumpet brings devastation to the earth itself
	2nd Trumpet (kazoo)	8:8-9	2nd trumpet is targeted towards the seas
	3rd trumpet (kazoo)	8:10-11	3rd trumpet affects the water supply which brings death to many
	4th trumpet (kazoo)	8:12	4th trumpet attacks the sky, affects sun, moon, and stars
	5th trumpet (kazoo)	9:1-12	5th trumpet releases Satan with power to use demonic influence, locusts, to torment those who have rejected God

Case#	Contents	Verse	Message
	6th trumpet (kazoo)	9:13-21	6th trumpet brings an astonishing amount of death.
	7th trumpet (kazoo)	11:15	7th trumpet is the announcement of Christ's reign is made as we move to the completion.
23	gold sash	1:9-20	Jesus as Judge & Priest
24	gemstones	21:19-20	foundations of heavenly city
25	plush lion	5:5	Jesus, the Lion of Judah to open the seals
26	plastic eyeball	1:1-7	every eye will see him
27	human face mask	4:7	around the throne singing worship
28	mouthwash	3:14-22	Spit you out Laodicea
29	wings (hair clip)	4:7	around the throne singing worship
30	plush lamb	5:6	Jesus
31	white horse cut-out	6:2	bent on conquest
	red horse cut-out	6:4	power to kill and make people kill
	black horse cut-out	6:5	holding scales (economic imbalance)
	pale (green) horse	6:8	Death
32	rocks	6:15-16	people hid from Jesus' judgment
33	tissue	21:4	God will wipe every tear
34	incense	8:3-4	people's prayers
35	bread crumbs	2:12-17	Pergamum
36	honey	10:9-10	taste of scroll
37	measuring stick	11:1	measure the temple
38	red dragon toy	12:1-17	Satan
39	leopard & bear toys	13:2	beast
40	fire - hot sauce	9:17-18	from mouths of horses
41	frog toys	16:13	false prophets
42	cinnamon & spices	18:13	cargo of merchants of the earth
43	flashlight	22:5	light only from God
44	black sun of felt	6:12	sixth seal with earthquake
45	palm branches (hand clapper)	7:9	people standing before the throne
46	plastic fruit	2:1-5	Love me as 1st (Ephesus)

Case#	Contents	Verse	Message
47	gold bowl	5:8 & 15:7	prayers and wrath
48	clay pots	2:27-28	rebellious shattered
49	seals (stickers)	5:1	scroll with seven seals
50	50 stickers	21:22-27	Lamb's Book of Life
51	red dragon & mini-nativity	12:3-5	beast and the woman
52	two crowns	4:9-11	crowns laid down
53	tissue	7:15-17	wipe every tear
54	plastic cow, frankincense & myrrh	18:11-13	Babylon's merchants
55	musical instrument	14:1-3	a new song
56	star & Hebrew tile	22:16	son of David, morning star
57	masks and rocks	6:14-15	rocks fall on us to hide from God
58	sporks, water, mac&cheese cup	3:19-20	come and dine with us
59	gold sun of foil	1:12-19	Jesus' face like the sun
60	oil and leaves	22:1-3	healing leaves from tree of life

Summary Activity: "Passport" to the Lord's "Diners Club" and our Journey Together to the Holy City.

The "Banker" is God offering participants eternal salvation if they will trade all their worldly possessions and wealth. For those willing, cases are traded for "passports to heaven" that contain a seal identifying them as one of God's chosen. (Commitment - Deal or No Deal? "I am a child of God to the end" - yes or no?) Participants place their cases in the middle in a pile and take a passport, writing their name inside.

Participants share their experience with the group.

In the first chapter of Genesis, as God was creating the earth, he said, "Let there be light." Since the creation of earth, we have lived by his sun during the day and his moon and stars during the night.

> *"Now the earth was formless and empty, darkness was over the surface of the deep, and the Spirit of God was hovering over the waters.*
>
> *And God said, "Let there be light," and there was light. God saw that the light was good, and he separated the light from the darkness.*

In Revelation 21 when Jesus returns, there will be no more need for earth's light, for the glory of God will be our light, and Jesus will be our lamp through which God's light will shine upon us. When God has completed all of creation and is finished with re-creation, we will walk solely in His light. Revelation 21:23 says:

> *And pray in the Spirit on all occasions with all kinds of prayers and requests. With this in mind, be alert and always keep on praying for all the Lord's people.*

Let us walk in His light.

Revelation 3:19-20

> *Those whom I **love** I rebuke and discipline. So be earnest and repent.*
> *20 Here I am! I stand at the door and knock. If anyone hears my voice and opens the door, I will come in and eat with that person, and they with me.*

Communion Invitation

At the last supper with his disciples, Jesus shared the bread and wine with them, and as he did, he shared his last parable, his last metaphors, before he was to be crucified. After all that Jesus had said and done to teach his disciples and to fulfill his prophecy of salvation, he wanted them to "completely consume" everything about him, to know that his body was to be broken and given for us and that his blood was to be poured out for us as a sign of the new covenant.

> *And he took bread, gave thanks and broke it, and gave it to them, saying, "This is my body given for you; do this in remembrance of me."* — Luke 22:19

> *In the same way, after the supper he took the cup, saying, "This cup is the new covenant in my blood, which is poured out for you.* — Luke 22:20

In modern language, he might have said something like, "I want you to eat, sleep, and breathe all that I am, all that the spirit of God is." Consume me and be consumed by me for your daily sustenance, for your physical, mental, and spiritual survival. Consume me. Let those who have ears to hear.

After Communion Elements are Consumed

In Matthew 13:9-17, Jesus said:

> *Whoever has ears, let them hear."*
>
> *The disciples came to him and asked, "Why do you speak to the people in parables?"*
>
> *He replied, "Because the knowledge of the secrets of the kingdom of heaven has been given to you, but not to them. Whoever has will be given more, and they will have an abundance. Whoever does not have, even what they have will be taken from them. This is why I speak to them in parables:*
>
> *"Though seeing, they do not see;*
> *though hearing, they do not hear or understand.*
>
> *In them is fulfilled the prophecy of Isaiah:*
> *"'You will be ever hearing but never understanding;*
> *you will be ever seeing but never perceiving.*
>
> *For this people's heart has become calloused;*
> *they hardly hear with their ears,*
> *and they have closed their eyes.*
> *Otherwise they might see with their eyes,*
> *hear with their ears,*
> *understand with their hearts*
> *and turn, and I would heal them.'*
>
> *But blessed are your eyes because they see, and your ears because they hear. For truly I tell you, many prophets and righteous people longed to see what you see but did not see it, and to hear what you hear but did not hear it.*

Closing Prayer

Lord God,

We give you all the praise, honor, and glory for who you are. You are the Alpha and Omega, the First and the Last. We praise you for your powerful yet gentle Holy Spirit.

We thank you for your Son, Jesus Christ, who died on the cross to save us from our sins and sinful natures. We are in awe of your everlasting grace and mercy, your compassion on us, your enduring patience toward the saved and unsaved.

We want to join the angels and saints in praising you around your throne in heaven, and we seek to lead a righteous life toward that end of spending eternity with you.

We thank you for your holy Word that speaks truth and faithfulness. We honor you for your eternal covenant to be our God and for us to be your people.

Come and dwell within our hearts and purify our souls so that we can be unified in your spirit and love.

We are forever grateful that you have created us, that you have instructed us, and that you have guided us to live each day with eyes to see, ears to hear, and hearts to feel your majesty, mercy, and greatness.

There is no one like you. May you be glorified and honored by all that we say and do. May we be made whole and holy in your sight! Until Jesus comes again, we say and sing, "Hallelujah! Amen! Come, Lord Jesus. Come!"

Closing Worship Song: "Come, Lord Jesus, Come" by Stephen McWhirter

"JOURNEY TOGETHER" SCRIPTURE AND REFLECTION ALONE IN YOUR ROOM

The prophecy of the Revelation of John is filled with really loud sounds. There are loud earthquakes, hail storms, thunder and lightning, and war between Satan and Jesus. There are verses describing continual loud praise and worship around the throne of God in heaven. In Chapter 21, when the new heaven and new earth appears, there is a loud shout of victory and peace?

> *And I heard a loud voice from the throne saying, "Look! God's dwelling place is now among the people, and he will dwell with them. They will be his people, and God himself will be with them and be their God. 'He will wipe every tear from their eyes. There will be no more death or mourning or crying or pain, for the old order of things has passed away."*
> — Revelation 21:3-4

However, there is one place in Revelation that describes a distinct time of complete silence in heaven around the throne of God. For "about half an hour", God suspends all the praise and worship filling heaven to receive "much incense" and "the prayers of all God's people." The smoke of the incense and the prayers of God's people rise up before God in complete silence. The reverence of the fragrant incense fills the altar as all God's attention is on our prayers.

Revelation 8:1-4

> ***When he opened the seventh seal, there was silence in heaven for about half an hour.***
>
> ***And I saw the seven angels who stand before God, and seven trumpets were given to them.***
>
> ***Another angel, who had a golden censer, came and stood at the altar. He was given much incense to offer, with the prayers of all God's people, on the golden altar in front of the throne. The smoke of the incense, together with the prayers of God's people, went up before God from the angel's hand.***

Our prayers could be written, spoken, sung, strummed, whispered, or shouted. Our prayers could be thanks, praise, requests, hurts, forgiveness, or any kind of communication with God. In whatever form we call on

God, he receives our prayers in silence and reverence. He wants us to know that by including this part in this prophecy.

Immediately following the silence is another noisy earthquake.

Take your time on this next part. Whatever has been your experience before coming to this retreat, and whatever may be waiting for you when you return home, take some time to consider about half an hour alone, in the silence, and reflect on your prayers to God that are rising to God's ears in the fragrance of incense reaching his senses.

Time is not linear for God, who always was, is, and always will be. However, for us, we deal with life in time segments. Find the time in your room this weekend to write down your prayers that you want to be taken directly before the throne of God. With the confidence of Scripture, the blood of the Lamb, and the faith of our testimony, we can trust that God cares about us, cares about our needs, and sets aside praise to himself from all the angels and saints in heaven to receive our prayers. Imagine that! Just for us!

Take your time. After you have written your prayers, or spoken your prayers, try misting your favorite perfume, or rubbing your hands with your favorite lotion or hand sanitizer, or anything with a pleasing aroma to you. Then close your eyes and imagine your prayers rising up to the throne of God in perfect silence with a focus on your words and feelings for him. Imagine your prayers rising, made stronger by incense of all the prayers of your friends and family and church family.

Breathe. Inhale the scent and imagine the Holy Spirit filling your lungs. Then exhale your prayers and imagine them flowing up with the air that you breathe out. Take your time. Your prayers have been heard, and they have been answered. Maybe you won't know when or how or where, but in God's timing, he has heard you and has answered you. Peace.

> *Amen! Come, Lord Jesus! May the grace of the Lord Jesus be with God's holy people."* — Revelation 22:20b-21

www.ingramcontent.com/pod-product-compliance
Lightning Source LLC
Chambersburg PA
CBHW051149120626
46547CB00012B/1004

* 9 7 9 8 9 8 5 6 9 8 8 8 6 *